Product Management:
Mastering the Product Role

Product Management: Mastering the Product Role

Asomi Ithia

Matador
9 Priory Business Park,
Wistow Road, Kibworth Beauchamp,
Leicestershire. LE8 0RX
Tel: 0116 279 2299
Email: books@troubador.co.uk
Web: www.troubador.co.uk/matador
Twitter: @matadorbooks

ISBN 978 1789018 769

British Library Cataloguing in Publication Data.
A catalogue record for this book is available from the British Library.

Printed and bound by CPI Group (UK) Ltd, Croydon, CR0 4YY
Typeset in 11pt Adobe Garamond Pro by Troubador Publishing Ltd, Leicester, UK

Matador is an imprint of Troubador Publishing Ltd

MIX
Paper from
responsible sources
FSC® C013604

To mum, passed but always here.
Thank you for giving us your love, care and attention

Contents

Acknowledgements

Many people have helped make this book possible – from speaking about their product management experiences and perspectives to listening to my thoughts and ideas, and providing feedback on the drafts. To each and every one, I say 'thank you' for giving up your time. It's with your input that this product exists.

Thank you to

Abdul Terry
Abisola Fatokun
Adam Warburton
Ahron Geminder
Ali Hussein
Alison Cusack
Allen Bastow
Amar Melwani
Andrew Rollason
Andy Black
Antoinette Lynch
Brendan Marry
Calvin Faife
Caspar Atkinson
Claire Hall
David Matthews
DC Patel
Denise Bennett
Diana Spiridon
Elisabeth Schloemmer
Gareth Capon
Garry Prior
James Gamble
James Routledge
Janna Bastow
Jas Ahluwalia
Joe Darkins

Jonathan Culling
Ken Kwabiah
Ladislav Bartos
Laura Nana
Leanne Cummings
Lester Bunn
Luca Vincenti
Manish Sahni
Marianna Satanas
Martin Ericsson
Michael Dargue
Michael Smith
Mike Darcy
Nick Charalambous
Nicky Hickman
Paul Cutter
Peter Bricknell
Peter McInally
Peter Newman
Peter Simon
Phoebe Innes-Wilson
Randy Silver
Rob Crook
Sabine Bickle
Sabine Capes
Stephen McDonald
Stuart Moore

Welcome

I'd like to share

Through the Product Management Series of 4 Books, I'd like to share product management thoughts and lessons gained from my experiences, and those of product practitioners and leading organisations.

The discipline of product management has seen significant change in its importance and application over the past 10+ years. Much of this has been driven by factors, such as increased customer power; a realisation that understanding and serving customer needs is critical to business success; the need to move quickly to maximise opportunities before someone else does or it disappears; new internet-age opportunities and business models; advancements in technology that make it easier to create products at scale, and changes in thinking about how organisations get work done.

Taking this into account, the purpose of the Product Management Series of books is to provide useful and thought-provoking insights that help product people, in mid to large organisations, get product management done in a pragmatic way that meets the needs of customers and the organisation.

Whether already deep in the product management trenches, or at the early stages of your career, the Product Management Series seeks to add to your knowledge and skills.

This book, **Product Management: Mastering the Product Role** opens with definitions of the business/customer value exchange, products, product management and its core and accompanying activities. The book goes onto outline a number of potential fits for product management in different organisational contexts. It then moves on to define product management roles, responsibilities, skills and competencies; provides guidance for being an effective product person; advice for nurturing and developing your product talent, and suggestions for engaging and working with stakeholders and making product management work in mid-to-large enterprises. Lastly, it covers a few thoughts on the future of product management and provides 2 tools for incrementally planning and reviewing progress.

Product Management Series – 4 Books for getting product management done

Combined with this book, the Product Management Series is designed to cover the spectrum of activities required to create, deliver and manage products that create value for your customers and business.

Product Management: Understanding Business Context and Focus covers how business context and focus relates to, and impacts, product management from the vision statement to goals, objectives, strategy, values and culture. It specifically looks at what each encompasses, different approaches organisations take to setting and implementation, and how this flows down to, and impacts, product management at a functional level.

Product Management: Bringing New Products to Market. Starting from framing the idea, this book encompasses setting a motivating vision, objectives and key performance indicators (KPIs); understanding customers and using this to create and deliver new products into market. Supporting areas that product people need to, as a minimum, understand and may need to get involved in defining and delivering, are also covered.

Product Management: Managing Existing Products. Beginning with questions that product people need to be able to answer, this book then goes through activities for creating a cadence for developing, optimising and executing strategies to move existing products forward – including objective setting, strategy and roadmaps, iterative delivery and much more.

Each book is laid out in a way that makes it easy to jump to particular topical areas. All areas of content are brought to life with constructs, figures, references and samples of experiences from product practitioners.

Customer and business needs

Businesses and customers have a co-dependency. Illustrated at the beginning of this book, this can be described as a bi-directional business/customer value exchange (or relationship) that delivers value to both.

As an important part of being in business, all books in the series aim to address this through covering the business and customer sides of product management, in equal measure. In short, a key theme of the books is to absolutely obsess about solving customer problems, but without losing focus or being apologetic about ensuring that the business achieves a return for its hard work.

Do it your way

We are all different, work differently and face situations that require different approaches. The books aim (as much as possible) to provide a flexible approach that includes options over a rigid set of rules, frameworks, or models.

Let me explain.

While meeting and interviewing product people for these books, one striking occurrence was the infrequency that they talked about frameworks or models. Most tended to just talk about how they 'got stuff done'. Here or there a model or framework would be mentioned, but in the main, more was said about ways of working and activities.

So, what does this mean for frameworks, models and constructs (of which the books contain a few)?

There is no doubt that they deliver immense value[i]. But not purely in a form that must be followed without deviation. When asked about frameworks and models, many of the people I interviewed had read about them, listened to people talk about them and been on training courses to learn about them. However, once past this learning, they either treat them as guides to help direct their work, pick parts to use when the need arises, or use them whole (when required).

In doing this, they have mastered the art of knowing when to use whole or parts of each – they have created their own approaches that work for their skills and context.

Effective product management is about continuously learning and challenging yourself to find new and better ways to deliver value – the books aim to support this by providing insights that help you build your knowledge and skill sets, and ultimately your own way to get product management done.

As you read, the content should be used as a guide that helps

---

i   As a minimum they provide a common reference point for coalescing around.

you understand key concepts and define your own approach. To support this, where possible, options have been added to help you select the path that is right for you, your organisation and context.

About me

I have been working in product management and product marketing for over 20 years in small and large businesses including BT, 02, Thomson Reuters, Sky and Barclays. In my time I have worked across all stages of the product lifecycle using a range of techniques to understand customer needs and deliver products against them – along the way I have experienced many ups and downs and never stopped learning. I have also had the opportunity to work with some great people, from whom I have learned so much (I know, it's a cliché, but very true).

Lastly, I co-host a product meet-up in London called The Product Group[ii]. It's a great place for topical debate, listening to product stories and meeting with great product people. I can also regularly be found at the monthly Product Tank[iii] events in London.

I hope you enjoy reading **Product Management: Mastering the Product Role** and find the series useful in your quest to get product done for your customers and business.

Asomi Ithia
www.asomiithia.com
www.productmanagementseries.com

---

ii   www.meetup.com/TheProductGroupLondon
iii   www.meetup.com/ProductTank

Introduction

Commercial organisations operate a business/customer value exchange: where the business offers value and in return the customer provides value.

From the customer's perspective, value equates to the business solving a problem[i]. The better the business accomplishes this the more value customers will return. From the businesses' perspective, value delivered to the customer must ultimately lead to profit, as David Packard said in the HP Way[1], "it is impossible to operate a business for long unless it generates a profit, and so if a company is to meet any of its other (customer, fields of interest, growth, employees, organisation citizenship) objectives, it must make a profit[ii].

In product management, it's easy to become obsessed with conversations around meeting customer needs[iii] to the extent

---

i   To try and simplify the use of terms (and save repeatedly writing 'needs/wants/problems'), this book describes customer problems as their needs and wants that are not being addressed effectively.

ii   Whether a commercial organisation or not-for-profit, all organisations need to generate a profit – defined as an amount of income that outstrips its costs. At one level so it can cover its costs and secondly so it can invest to develop.

iii Much of this is understandable as a means to redress a historical bias towards profit over customer problems.

that business value is forgotten. However, ultimately without profit there is no business and as the people at HubSpot[2] wrote, "bankrupt companies don't delight customers".

In the business/customer value exchange product management is the discipline and vehicle for creating and managing products that deliver value to the business and customer.

Great product management (and indeed business management) is a virtuous cycle of value exchange that rewards both sides: customers with products that help them solve their problems and businesses with ongoing returns that reward their efforts for solving the customer's problem.

Core to product management's ability to contribute to the value exchange is a clear understanding of business objectives from which product objectives and strategy are set: product objectives being the target outcomes (1) that need to be achieved as a result of delivering value to customers, and strategy (2) being the mechanism for understanding customers' needs and creating

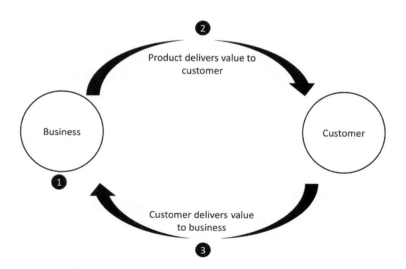

Figure 1: Business/Customer Value Exchange

products that address them, which in turn delivers value from the customer to the business (3) (figure 1).

To arrive at an optimum value exchange, product people need to deeply understand customer problems and use this insight to continuously create, deliver and optimise products.

Mastering the product role seeks to support product people and teams through this cycle by covering topical areas that need to be thought about and delivered against in order to get the product job done.

1

Product and Product Management

Product management is about becoming wedded to the customer problem, and not the solution. This delineation frees the mind to focus on continuously creating, delivering, managing and canning products (and features) in search of the best product for your customer's.

The product management domain encompasses the combined product experiences that span customer interactions from initial engagement to last usage – at a very high level these experiences can be categorised as pre-engagement, engagement, use and disengagement (figure 2).

A more detailed breakdown of the end-to-end experience may cover categories, such as product information gathering (research and learning); finding, assessing, selecting, purchasing or signing up to the product (search, select and buy); receiving or accessing the product (get); using the product (use); accessing support when a question or problem arises (help & support), and renewing or ending use of the product (retain/cancel/lapse).

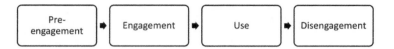

Figure 2: High Level Product Experience Categories

Bringing this to life with the experience for a news app serving users need to stay up-to-date with the latest news. The experience might start with a search of the internet to find a news app that can complete the job (research); before then going to the organisation's site or an app store to read more about it e.g. availability, news coverage, cost etc. (learning). Once satisfied that the news app can deliver, next comes the download (and maybe paying, if it's a subscription based app) from the app store (search, select, buy and get). Now the value starts to be realised through multiple options to access news e.g. categories, personalised feeds, notifications and the ability to share interesting content via messaging or social media platforms (use). If help is required this can be found in context, via a webpage or in a user group or forum (help and support). When a new version of the app is launched, it can be updated in the background or via a simple onscreen request. If it is no longer useful it can be uninstalled (cancel).

When creating and managing products, product people need to know about the core elements of the experience and the wrap of additional elements required to make it complete. In essence, product people need to know a lot about a lot and something about some things – what fits into each camp will depend on the product and organisation.

To make product management happen, a huge part of the function is to bring together multiple strands and people to create a cohesive whole. As Ken Norton[3] wrote, "product management is the glue that holds together all the various functions and roles across a company that speak different languages".

Let's get into these areas.

2

Core and accompanying activities

To deliver, product management must engage in a number of core and accompanying activities (figure 3).

Core activities focus on vision, goals and objectives, understanding the customer's problems, then creating and optimising products that meet those needs. Accompanying activities focus on all the wrap around activities that complete the end-to-end experience.

Using the term 'accompanying' is not to downplay the importance of these, more to call out that responsibility and expertise in these areas are less likely to be in the product management team. This makes them areas that product people must know about, but not necessarily as a core part of the role – more on this later.

Having multiple areas of work cross paths illustrates the beauty and beast of product management. Beauty as it touches so many different activities, and beast as it requires you to be a generalist in many areas.

Figure 3: Core and Accompanying Product Management Activities

As product people, it's crucial to understand and think about each of these areas. You could, for instance, create a new app-based service that enables customers to seamlessly purchase items 24/7/365. However, if the item is not delivered as promised you've failed to deliver the experience your customer expected.

Core activities

Creating, delivering and managing a product requires a team effort across multiple activities and areas of the organisation. Central to this is understanding the business context and focus; creating the product vision, goals, objectives and strategy, then executing against this. All these activities follow and require the deepest level of knowledge and focus for product management.

Business context and focus. Understanding the business vision, goals, objectives and strategic focus and how they translate into expectations and requirements of the product.

Product vision and objectives. Using the business context and focus to set the product aims and aspirations, targets and measurements.

Product strategy. Defining the customer problem and using this to shape the product.

Product creation. Creating the product through activities such as customer journey mapping, experience design, concept creation, user testing, delivery and management.

Product growth, development and removal. Managing the early stages of the in-life product from fixing bugs to optimising and adding new features, then scaling and growing it in line with demand and the product objectives, before eventually removing it from the market (ideally to be replaced by a stepped changed product).

Accompanying activities

Accompanying activities are numerous and important to create a great end-to-end product experience for your customers. Of primary interest for product people are business case/pitch, budgets, pricing, customer communications, sales and distribution, customer service and support, operations, partnering and internal communications.

Business case/pitch. Creating and seeking approval and investments to move forward at different stages of the product's lifecycle. Including objectives, Key Performance Indicators (KPIs) and strategy, proposition, funding, budgets, financial model, delivery plan.

Budgets. Creating financial plans that detail required investment and returns over a period of time (depending on the set-up). This can include demonstrating outcomes to gain future investment.

Pricing. Creating and adjusting the product price.

Customer communications. Creating and executing promotional activities to drive product uptake and retention.

Sales and distribution. Selling and delivery through off and online channels.

Customer services and product support. Setting up and evolving product support capabilities from minimal operational support to full support models.

Operations. Creating, delivering and executing support activities that underpin all activities e.g. legal (contracts, terms and conditions), procurement (purchase agreements), finance (budgeting and financial models), project management and delivery support.

Partnering. Developing partnerships and channels for acquiring product (e.g. value add stuff or commercial partners), selling and distributing the product.

Internal communications[iv]. Creating and executing employee communication activities to ensure knowledge and engagement with the organisations greatest advocates.

In mid to large organisations, many of these activities are delivered (or heavily supported) by dedicated teams that product people need to engage and work with. On occasion product will need to cover some of these activities, however your primary interest should be

---

iv   This is borderline (a core vs accompanying activity) and you should expect to be the primary driver of internal communications, seeking expertise from your internal comms team for advice and support to communicate your message.

a conversational understanding of what they are and how they fit in the product picture. In the book **Product Management: Bringing New Products to Market** each of the accompanying activities is covered in terms of what product people need to know and may need to do.

3

Organisational fit

Ample is written about the role of product in relation to the core activities (and more broadly in the organisation). Much of this talks about the product team or person as leading and driving decisions about the product (the term 'mini-CEO' comes to mind). Today, it is not quite so simple and the role product people play in these areas can vary from organisation to organisation.

An analysis of personal experiences and those of other product people leads to 4 descriptions of the product role fit in mid-to-large organisations: influential leader (leads through ability and need to influence individuals and teams), follower (takes direction from the overall business owner or lead), collaborator (works jointly with peers, seeking guidance from a leader with little or no affiliation to a particular business area) and leaders in charge (leads on setting the direction and strategy for teams to follow).

Influential leader

Product leads and drives the product strategy and decisions using influence and negotiation to gain input, buy-in and execution

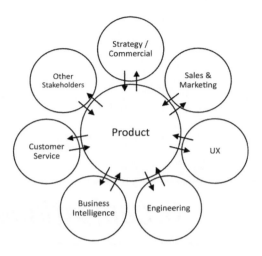

Figure 4: Influential Leader

support from key stakeholders (figure 4). Or as a Head of Product said, "you're the steering wheel of the car. A car that is made up of multiple parts (teams) that you need to steer in the right direction".

In this instance, the product person typically starts with input from business strategy and other key stakeholders, before headlining the product strategy and getting a wider group of stakeholders involved for validation and delivery support.

At a media company, this was the case when a major new product was to be launched. A newly appointed Head of Product was given the responsibility for driving forward the product strategy (from proposition to live) and bringing together various parts of the organisation to support delivery. Although each business area had its local expertise, it was the responsibility of the Head to ensure that they were all aligned to create a seamless experience – if one or more of these did not fit, then they would be asked why!

At another media company, when launching a new transactional site, product defined the strategy and then worked to garner the input and support from multiple teams of domain experts (e.g. content, user experience (UX), sales, marketing, technology etc.) to execute the strategy. Without the input of these experts the site would not have been delivered.

Facebook[4] illustrates this well in describing the product person and role as, "visionaries who guide new product ideas from an initial concept to a full-blown product launch. Along the way, we collaborate with world-class engineers and designers to maximise each product's impact on the world".

Follower

Product strategy decisions are taken by other stakeholders (typically commercial, strategy, sales, marketing, business development or senior management) from whom product takes its direction and follows in an execution or delivery role (figure 5).

Four scenarios reflect product in the follower role.

Figure 5: Follower

One: product strategy, proposition or opportunity is owned by another team. At a currency exchange company, the opportunity and strategy (including market analysis etc.) was defined by the commercial team and handed to the product team, who then became responsible for executing and maximising the opportunity. The strategy included the market analysis, the value proposition and decisions on key elements of the product.

At a media company launching a product in a new market, the strategy team provided the direction (including defining the target market, market position and criteria for entering), an external agency identified and specified the target customer, the marketing team defined the proposition (including a value statement, price and product types) and promotion plan, leaving the product team to define the customer experience and product features (with input from the strategy team). Similarly, I was once presented with and asked to execute, a product strategy for an integration with a partner's platform.

Two: product is one part of an overall proposition that is owned by another team. For instance, at the same media company, there were multiple products sitting under an overall proposition. Here, the proposition owner defined the overall product strategy, with the product team responsible for delivering in line with that. While in a telecoms company, the marketing team owned the overall proposition and the physical and online product teams worked to deliver in line with the marketing proposition.

Three: capability supports and is embedded in another product. In one company, the search team owned and managed the search capability. However, as an enabling service, it had to align with the strategies of the products consuming its capabilities. Similarly, an identity service that enables customers to access multiple products across the company's estate was required to meet the needs and fit the strategies of those products.

Four: product is helping a business area that does not have product management capabilities deliver its offerings as a product. An example might be a customer service team delivering a new mobile app, a sales team launching an internal lead tracking site or a HR team launching an app or site to support its recruitment efforts. Being a follower may not be an ideal state for product people, although in most instances there is scope for product to use their expertise to influence and lead the direction of the core underlying product.

Collaborator

Product works in collaboration with key stakeholders and domain experts as equal partners to decide and agree on the product strategy and execution plan (figure 6).

Stakeholders who sit at the top table, typically include strategy, commercial, sales and marketing, subject matter experts and product (plus, more recently UX and engineering). Given that the teams are collaborating, they are likely to be led by a business sponsor or general manager whose role is to set the overall direction and facilitate

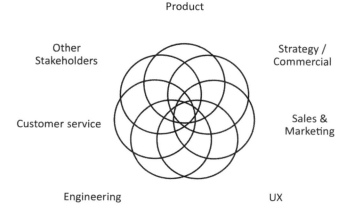

Figure 6: Collaborator

collaboration between the teams. In some organisations, a sponsor or general manager is not present and teams will natively collaborate as equal partners e.g. GitHub, Gore-Tex and Valve where people have more freedom and scope to pick and choose what they work on.

An anecdote from an executive described a scenario whereby the business took a decision to create a product steering committee that shared ownership and overall responsibility for the product strategy. In the committee, that included representation from strategy, sales and marketing, engineering and finance, product management's role was to run the process – from bringing together the teams to guiding the debate, reaching agreement on the strategy[v], creating a cohesive plan and driving delivery.

At a progressive insurance company, teams came together to deliver mini initiatives that were backed by senior management. Each initiative had a business sponsor, whose primary role was to set the context and direction. Outside of this it was down to the members to jointly agree the targeted outcomes and approach. This meant that although product teams led most of the initiatives, any other team could lead an initiative.

In each initiative, the collaborators are considered domain experts that will contribute and make decisions about their respective areas. So, for example, when aiming to increase the products offered to customers, everyone (commercial, product, customer service, technology, UX, analytics, etc.) gathered for a kick-off session to discuss options and the approach that would be taken. Each person contributed to the overall discussion and also used their domain expertise to headline areas for consideration or concern. At the end the solution was agreed and each person took actions that related to their domain.

---

v   A none too easy task, especially when there are different (sometimes clashing) perspectives at the table e.g. strategy's focus on the long-term, sales and marketing's focus on the short term, engineering's focus on technical capabilities and what's new, and finance's focus on cost and return on investments.

In an example from a gaming company, product ideation sat in marketing. Shaping the ideas and working with the UX and engineering teams to deliver, sat with product, and pricing, 3rd party deals and Profit & Loss (P&L) sat with the commercial team. In other instances, product shares overall responsible with SMEs (Subject Matter Experts), e.g. in the finance and insurance field). Here the SME brings their technical or industry knowledge and expertise, while the product person brings customer understanding and product development expertise.

Collaborative approaches work well where there is great cohesion and respect for the value that each participant brings to the group or where areas of responsibility are clearly defined and respected – the former being the better situation.

Leader in charge

Product drives all the core product decisions (figure 7) and heavily influences (to the point of directing) the decisions in support areas.

Figure 7: Leader in Charge

Product as the leader in charge is more likely to occur where the product is the core focus that other areas are tasked with servicing and supporting. As opposed to instances where the product is the vehicle for delivering the core asset. Take an organisation like Microsoft, its products are core and fundamental to the company's existence. Whereas for a media organisation, such as the BBC, its digital products (site, apps, player etc.) are used to deliver its core offering of content.

Product as the leader in charge can also be found where the product is not a core offering and therefore does not have a focal light shone on it and therefore product management gets to call all the shots. A dichotomous situation, in that the product people have all the say, but as it's not core it may be side stepped for investment in favour of the focal products. I once worked on a product that had a bit of both in that it was a non-sexy enabling capability, and therefore as long as it worked I was left to drive it forward and lead all aspects.

For any product, product management may play a dual role. For instance, the role may be to meet the proposition owners' needs (as a follower) while developing deep product insight and a capability that allows it to be a best in class product (as a leader). I once worked in a situation where other team's product strategies drove a lot of our work, while sitting alongside this we had our own parallel strategy to ensure that the overall product was developing and improving – especially in areas that other teams did not think (and/or care) about.

As the above illustrates, there are a number of different situations being played out today. As, for a multitude of reasons, each organisation is different and will divide responsibilities based on the org structure, P&L ownership, subject matter expertise, board representation, history, and of course power bases (unfortunately!).

It should also be noted that contexts where the product person is playing more of a follower role, may not be so bad. For example, if it means the product gets fully funded because it is closely aligned to a revenue line owned by sales, then this could be better than having to beg, steal, borrow and justify every decision to a sceptical funding committee that has little interest in the product's success. For many product people, the ideal scenario is to, at least, play the influential leader or collaborator role (and avoid the follower role). However, as the above illustrates this may not be the case until the product role gains more traction and understanding in organisations.

As product moves forward and makes polite (or hand banging) demands over its role, it's important to understand the context and history of the organisation and work from there to establish the right footing for product. Especially, as historically, even though they did not have the word 'product' in their titles, other roles (e.g. strategy, commercial, sales or marketing people) may have been responsible for all or parts of the activities we now consider primary to product management.

To get to and/or maintain the influential leader or collaborator role, product must continue to (or in some instances, start to) educate the organisation and prove its value. Modern technology companies, such as Google, Yahoo, Netflix, Facebook, Just Eat, Ocado etc. have always had a product presence at the highest levels and can be used as a shining light for other organisations. While companies, such as Sky, Adobe, Experian, Channel 4, Legal & General, Paddy Power, Sage and Tesco can be used to demonstrate the value at executive levels in established organisations.

Supporting this movement, organisations, including Facebook, Twitter, Google, HubSpot, TripAdvisor, Box, Amazon and Drobox to name a few, are also running leadership programs based on product roles.

Using these and other examples, it's product's job to share experiences and successes and, more importantly, continuously demonstrate why it has such an important role to play within the organisation.

Going further, to gain or cement the leader in charge role, product needs to learn about the other areas of the business and be able to show leadership in them – again this is being addressed in the leadership programmes. And is something you can do as you develop your product career.

With this in mind, books **Product Management: Bringing New Products to Market** and **Product Management: Managing Existing Products** are written from the perspective of the product person, playing at least the influential leader or collaborator role – as this is where the consensus feels the product role should be now.

4

Roles, responsibilities and competencies

Product management time can broadly be split between strategic and tactical activities, the former focusing on thinking about and defining the bigger picture for the product. While the latter focuses on delivering against the strategy. It goes without saying that the more senior the role the more time that will be spent on strategy and helping direct reports develop and achieve (figure 8).

Across this spectrum, most product management roles cover 4 levels[vi]: manager/owner, senior/head of, director and chief[vii]. As indicated in figure 9, there is overlap between levels of role and some organisations will merge the responsibilities of 2 roles into one.

---

vi   At the entry level, there are the associate or junior roles which should be considered as early stage versions of the manager/owner roles, while at the most senior level the chief level roles can extend onto the executive team.

vii In terms of naming conventions, Chief Product Office and Director, Head of, Senior, Manager, Junior, Associate and Executive are the most common titles. However, there are other variations such as SVP, VP, Global Product Manager, Technical Product Manager, Product Designer, Product Specialist, Product Development Manager etc.

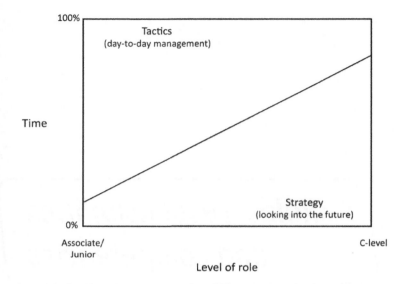

Figure 8: Role Level & Division of Time

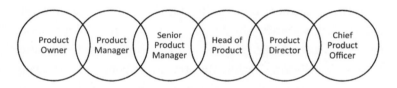

Figure 9: Overlapping Product Roles

Product manager and owner

Very closely aligned are the product manager and product owner roles. In some instances they are interchangeable and it is not clear how or if the 2 are different. By thinking about upstream (customer and stakeholder facing) and downstream (development focused) responsibilities, it is possible to describe and represent the 2 roles standalone and working alongside each other.

Upstream responsibilities

- Understand the business context and focus and align the product to this
- Create the product vision, objectives, strategy and roadmap incl. proposition development, business cases and KPIs
- Be the domain expert and product evangelist
- Create and communicate a product story that your team and stakeholders can and do buy into
- Be the customer advocate that continuously places the customer at the heart of all product decisions
- Develop deep customer, product and domain knowledge and expertise incl. capturing and understanding customer, market and competitor trends and analysis, and use this to create commercial opportunities
- Develop and manage an outcome-led roadmap that results in continuous product enhancements that deliver against the product vision and objectives
- Use user research techniques to create draft products and features e.g. wires, mock-ups etc.
- Set-up and run experiments to identify opportunities to enhance the customer experience and deliver against objectives
- Capture and analyse internal and external data to support decision making
- Collaboratively work with and engage the core team (incl. engineering and UX) and stakeholders (incl. sales/business development, marketing, partners, suppliers, communities, etc.) to create and deliver end-to-end solutions to customer problems
- Identify, engage, manage, influence, chivvy along and collaborate with stakeholders
- Openly communicate with the team and all stakeholders
- Develop material and kits to support sales and marketing
- Report on product performance to the team and stakeholders
- Manage requests, investment and tracking of product budgets

- Manage 3rd party partner and supplier relationships
- Project management

Downstream responsibilities

- Lead requirement gathering and write user stories, manage the product backlog incl. writing cards, prioritising, setting release cycles, running stand-ups, leading planning games, showcases and retrospectives
- Run experiments and work with experimentation techniques such as A/B and multi-variant testing to identify scalable solutions to customer problems
- Capture and interpret customer and product insights and use to drive the product forward
- Use data, insights and metrics to make sense of the incomprehensible, solve problems, drive and support decision making
- Investigate opportunities, issues and problems and lead the team to a resolution
- Work with Agile methodologies
- Understand the technology stack and its core components across all platforms
- Supplier management
- Manage the use of budgets development budgets
- Manage delivery plans and timelines

If there is one product manager or owner, then they will complete both up and downstream activities. However, if there is one of each, I would expect the product manager to complete the upstream activities, while the downstream activities will sit with the product owner[viii] (figure 10).

---

viii If a product manager and owner are working alongside each other, some overlap in activities should be expected – you need to work out which and how you minimise duplication.

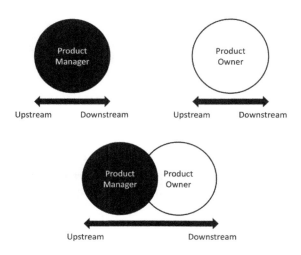

Figure 10: Upstream and Downstream Product Activities and Roles

Whether product manager or owner[ix], in order to effectively complete these activities, you must have the following skills and competencies:

- Bias for action
- Can do attitude
- Curious, investigative and learning mind
- Data driven and analytical
- Problem solver
- Stakeholder management
- Commercial acumen
- People skills
- Communication
- Influence and persuasion

---

ix   I was once asked which one I think is more important if there is only one role. In simple terms I would say the product manager role as in its more formal description it covers up and downstream activities. While the product owner role emanated from software development teams and has a stronger leaning towards the development side of product management.

- Ability to sell an idea
- Flexibility and adaptability
- Be able to make a decision and stand by it
- Emotional intelligence and empathy
- Technical expertise or at least knowledge and understanding

Looking at the product manager role, McKinsey[5] has developed a useful product manager maturity assessment that calls out 6 areas of capability (customer experience, market orientation, business acumen, technical skills, soft skills and enabling) that all product people should be skilled in.

Decisions about which role (product manager, product owner or both) is most appropriate, need to start by thinking about the task to be completed – once finished the job role(s) should be designed . For instance, if the role requires a lot of time to be spent away from the team (say with partners or working with stakeholders), then a separate product owner role should be considered. Whereas if the role means the same person can manage the end-to-end process on their own, then one person with either job title (preferably product manager) should be sufficient.

If the work is ample, consideration should go beyond trying to make do by stretching people to manage both (for example constantly asking someone (the BA) to be a quasi-product manager to cover). Here you should look at realigning the product into small enough chunks that one person can complete – the book **Product Management: Managing Existing Products** looks at a number of options for product set-up.

Role descriptions and responsibilities are a useful starting point, however no 2 product jobs are the same and job descriptions never quite describe how your time will be split. You need to understand this and define the role(s) accordingly.

Research, such as that conducted by Alpha UX[6], identified that product people spend their time (in order of where most time is spent) meeting with stakeholders, talking to customers, navigating internal politics, crafting roadmaps, running experiments, writing user stories and keeping up with best practices.

In terms of the most prevalent product manager responsibilities, the research identified the following: setting roadmap (76%), writing user stories (71%), customer interviews (59%), managing development team (50%), A/B testing (41%), prototyping (40%), hiring (26%), revenue targets (26%) and P&L (23%).

Latched onto (and not explicit in job descriptions) should be the time spent dealing with internal politics, fighting for resources, meetings (sometimes copious amounts of them), fixing or trying to work with broken internal processes, burdensome regulations and legacy platforms. To name but a few things lurking in the corridors of many organisations.

So you don't lose the will to do product here are some smart ideas people have used to get product done.

Adel Shehadeh[7] suggests, "not freaking out". "Ideas and suggestions" will come from multiple sources (including customers and internal stakeholders) and "your role is to calm down, absorb these suggestions, think them through and filter only the meaningful ones. While keeping everybody happy".

Talking about one of the weekly product management meetings to discuss practices and experiences, Arielle Silverman[8] said, "today we talked about pairing with designers. It was a good conversation. I especially liked talking about how we collaborate with designers in usability testing sessions".

Describing the Monday training slot, Anne-Sophie Lardet[9] talked about how on one occasion they brought "the team up to speed on new features and show them the updated version of the roadmap".

Yee Lee[10] talks about hosting a "'bug bash' (internal bug-finding party), kind of a quick dogfooding[x] for the latest feature to reach code complete." And a "check in with product and execs to get sign-off for deployment of new features".

---

x   Tech slang for working out the glitches

Senior product manager and head of product

Moving to the senior product manager or head of product roles, the responsibilities increase as does the expectation of the person in role.

Senior product managers and heads of must be able to:

- Lead a team of product people to achieve across one product or a product portfolio
- Create and develop a product capability that is able to continuously deliver products
- Support the teams work by opening doors and building relationships that benefit the team
- Mentor, coach and develop direct reports

As illustrated in 'Figure 8: Role Level & Division of Time' at the beginning of this section, these roles will swap some tactical activities for those that are more strategic and people orientated. In most organisations, they will likely engage in overseeing and/ or delivering some, or all, of the product manager activities listed above – even where managing a team of people, a wise person will still keep their finger on the pulse with projects and initiatives that complement their teams work.

In terms of skills and competencies, you should hold the same as a product manager, plus be able to:

- Think strategically whilst also rolling up your sleeves to get the job done
- Lead, manage and develop the team
- Communicate up, down, across and outside the organisation
- Motivate yourself and the team to achieve

Depending on the organisation structure, from this level up the product role may also be responsible for managing business analysts, researchers, UX/UI designers, product marketers, data analysts and scientists and (sometimes) engineers.

Nestled in and around the head of and senior product manager roles is the principle product manager. A role that Amazon has been using for a number of years and is now spreading to other organisations. Principle product managers take a lead role in their business area and are very much focused on the vision and strategy side of product management.

As a former Amazon employee[11] stated, "Amazon has PMs at 3 levels – L5 is PM, L6 is Senior PM, L7 is Principal PM. The next level up is L8 which is Director".

Product director

Increasing in strategic focus, the product director should give up all their execution activities (or at least a significant portion) and take on an overseeing and directional role with their team.

Product directors must be able to:

- Use data and insights to create and deliver short, mid and long-term product objectives and strategies that are aligned to business strategy
- Communicate and achieve buy-in for strategies within their own team and across the organisation
- Champion the product portfolio across the industry
- Own and drive forward the Profit & Loss (P&L) for the product portfolio
- Provide direction, lead and nurture a team of senior product people to deliver results across a product portfolio
- Focus the team on being customer-obsessed while achieving commercial success
- Create a team that continuously delivers beyond expectations
- Remove blockers, so that the team can stay focused on what's important

- Create strong and collaborative relationships with other business leaders and units
- Understand customers' problems first-hand by getting involved

In order to effectively complete these activities, they must have the following skills and competencies:

- Vision
- Strategic thinking
- Leadership
- Analytical
- Flexibility and adaptability to change
- Integrity
- Communication
- Influencing
- Ability to delegate and achieve through their team
- Trustworthy, open, transparent and empathetic
- Positive motivator

Chief Product Officer

Moving to the next level, the responsibilities again increase and require a more global strategic head and long-term view across the organisation, plus the ability to oversee multiple streams of work within and outside the team.

Chief Product Officers (CPOs) must have all the attributes of a product director, plus be able to:

- Set and lead the overall vision, objectives and strategy for the product group
- Lead and provide direction to the senior product leadership team (which in turn filters through to the whole product management function)

- Provide input into the broader business vision, goals, objectives and strategy
- Represent product management at the executive level incl. sharing and communicating product performance updates and plans
- Lead and influence at all levels of the organisation
- Sponsor, lead and support cross-functional product initiatives
- Create ways of working that significantly contribute to building and evolving the culture of the team and whole organisation

In order to effectively complete these activities, they must have the same skills, competencies and aptitudes as the product director, with the ability to use these skills at an executive level inside and outside the organisation.

Aligned to 'Figure 8: Role Level and Division of Time' at the beginning of this section, CPOs will not spend any time completing hands-on product work. Although, you would expect them to engage in activities that ensure they are able to stay in touch with the customer's view of the world and product.

Shifting up levels

As you move across these roles, activities are substituted, so the more senior the role the broader the coverage, the more strategic and the more it is about sharing a vision and leading products and people.

In terms of qualifications, manager and head of levels will require at least a degree (in some organisations an MBA is preferred), while senior directors and CPOs will likely need to have a masters. However, the reality is that in many instances, especially the more senior levels, experience will trump qualifications and companies will not overlook someone who has 10 years' experience operating at a senior level.

On the experience side, this becomes more important as the seniority of the role increases. Many senior roles will either look for 7+ years' experience in product management, consulting or related business areas.

One of the big callouts across roles are the leadership skills required to compliment the specific role-based skills and competencies. Asked the question, you would expect that leadership skills are required more as the role increases in seniority. However, as research conducted by HBR, Zenger and Folkman[12] suggests, leadership skills, such as the ability to inspire and motivate; high integrity and honesty; problem solving; a drive for results; powerful and proficient communication; collaboration and relationship building are fundamentals at all role levels (figure 11).

Zenger and Folkman found that, "as people move up the organisation, the fundamental skills they need will not dramatically change".

If you have plans for moving up start developing and honing these skills now, they will help you now and in the future.

In summing up product roles, they can be quite diverse from company to company. However if there are a few key areas

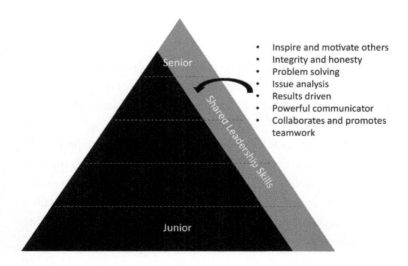

Figure 11: Shared Leadership Skills at all Levels of Product Management

that product people of all levels should have a strong grasp of, these are (in no particular order): a focus on understanding and meeting the needs of the customer; the ability to capture and use data and insight to support decision making; understanding of what strategy is (relative to the role) and the ability to set and execute it; ability to create and manage a roadmap; domain knowledge and expertise that helps drive not only data driven decisions, but also intuition (can be gained when in post); excellent knowledge and understanding of internet technologies; knowledge of Agile principles and methodologies; a persuasion for collaborative working; ability to lead and influence direct team and stakeholders; communication skills, whether up, down, sideways or external; people management and motivation skills (especially in more senior roles); ability to think big, think the impossible; a commercial savviness that balances customer and business needs, and the ability to succinctly tell and evangelise your products' story.

So there you have it, the main product roles. What great roles. What a fantastic array of activities, skills and competencies. What fantastic opportunities to deliver real value to customers and the business.

5

Being an effective product person

Going beyond the requirements of a job specification, each organisation and (hiring person) will seek a set of skills and competencies that are nuanced to them and their organisation. To be the best you can be there are a number that you can develop and nurture to place yourself in the best position for success.

Effective you

Get the basics right

When Leicester City won the English Premier League in 2016, it wasn't because they decided to create an intricate way of playing football. It was because they went back to basics and got these right. The same for product management, the basics will provide the foundational piece that enables you to be successful.

High on the list of basics is really caring about the product and the problem it is aiming to address. Without this everything else that you do will be lacklustre and devoid of the right level of motivation to do well for the customer, your business and, of course, yourself.

As you go through the remainder of this section, consider all of the topics covered here to be the product management basics.

Be curious

Children are encouraged to ask questions as a means to learn what they don't know. When we reach adulthood there are still things we don't know. However, a lot of the time we stop asking questions, exploring and investigating.

Ask questions, be curious, explore, discover and analyse new things that will help you better understand your customers, your competitors, the markets you operate in, the people you work with, the way you work, the technologies you use, and many other phenomena that surround the world of product management.

Be a storyteller

Much of the success of your product will ride on you and your teams' ability to communicate what it is you are trying to achieve. So, always have your product story front of mind and be able to communicate it inside and outside your team – think corridor conversation where you have 15 seconds to explain your product and leave the listener wanting to know more.

Make decisions

One of the areas frequently discussed by product people is how to make (the right) product decisions. From selecting the right strategy and execution plan to selecting and prioritising items for the roadmap, setting budgets, deciding on experiments, etc. etc. product people face lots of decisions points.

Unfortunately, there is no silver bullet answer that says that when you have X decision to make, the answer is Y. And in most situations there are going to be multiple choices that are credible.

However, at those decision points, it is important that you are able to decide and stand by your decision.

At these decision points it is important to gather the facts, assimilate them, take a decision and act on that decision. Or to use a military approach observe, orientate, decide and act (OODA). OODA is an especially useful example as it was first used to support fighter pilots who had to make snap decisions while in the heat of battle. From a product perspective, it should teach us that with the right mindset timely decisions can be made given the right considerations. The only additional factor to add would be a risk assessment element that enables you to gauge the risk and potential impact as a means to help decide on the best action.

Be bold

Don't be afraid to take a different route if you need to. If you need to take a different course to get to where you want to, take it. Goals and objectives should remain relatively static, while your strategy and tactics can change especially if new information says you should or need to. However, don't become the chaotic person that starts and never finishes anything because you are continuously exercising the right to take a different route. Keep evaluating your priorities and change when you need to.

Use your intuition and gut instinct. Scientists[13] are starting to prove that your gut instinct and intuition is driven by a brain in your stomach that "communicates back and forth with the brain in our heads", which in turn drives our instinctive feelings in some situations. Learn how to use this to support calculated risk-taking. You'll be surprised by how much you know, that you did not know you knew.

Get stuff done

Strategies, ideas and plans are great, and to get these agreed can be considered an achievement. However, the real achievement is in the execution and delivery. We all know that without great execution, the best strategies can go begging and deliver nothing. Or as Satya Patel[14] wrote, "potentially nothing is more important for PMs than the ability to just get sh*t done. No amount of insight compensates for an inability to help team's ship products".

And as a head of product so candidly put it, "deal with sh*t, as sh*t happens every day".

Say no

It isn't always easy, but without saying no, you will be run ragged and over the course of time you will lose focus and stop delivering.

Techniques for saying no range from the blunt, "No" to the "No, because of ABC (a rational explanation)". Both have their place, use them.

Communicate

Communicate, communicate, communicate, and over-communicate. Brands show people adverts 10-20 times in order to deliver their message. Your product message is no different and it will take people a few times of hearing it to fully engage. So tell 'em, tell 'em again and tell 'em again, and don't worry about the people who forget the first (or second) time, tell 'em again or change how you tell them so it resonates.

Share information and insight

Be the router for your product information and share everything that is relevant with the right people. In a collaborative environment 'knowledge sharing' is power as when it's in the right hands amazing things can happen.

Seek feedback

Ask for it and use what you receive to improve your product, yourself, your team, your processes and ways of working. Balance your 'asks' between the people you know support you and the detractors, both could help you see things you have missed.

Know what you don't know and ask

No one knows everything, even domain experts. So you don't need to play like you know everything. When you don't know and guess it may only take you in the wrong direction, especially if you are the domain expert that people rely on. So it's important to know when to ask and where to go to find the answer.

Be comfortable not knowing

But find someone or do something to get to know (e.g. run a test or experiment or do some research or speak to an expert).

With so much information and change, the world is more ambiguous than ever. Embrace this ambiguity and the fact that new information and insights will always be making their way towards you. Plan for change and leave scope to be able to use new information to support a change in direction, refinement or challenge of an idea – ambiguity will only work against you if you are set in your ways and do not see the possibilities to do things differently.

Be self-aware (especially what you're not good at)

Many of us would like to be gold medallists at everything. But we're not and won't be. Recognise what you are good at and find people or create teams with a balance that helps get all the things we need done.

Be humble, passionate and confident

Enough said.

Have thick skin

Social media illustrates that no matter what you think there will always be someone who thinks differently to you. Not only this, they are prepared to let you know. Interactions with stakeholders may not go to the extremes that can be found in social media, however there will be people who don't agree with you and express this in a forthright way. As the person who spends a lot of time in the middle of the crowd (of stakeholders) you need to prepare to hear things that may cause your skin to itch. Unfortunately, it's part of the job.

Sometimes it will be unreasonable and frankly out of order and other times it will hit you in a way that you did not expect, by being true.

Having thick skin will help you repel the initial shock, after which review the comments and decide what to do: change you, change how you work or ignore the comment as the person was just trying to cause you discomfort. Being self-aware and having a mentor may help to rationalise some of these instances (more on this later).

Continuously learn and be adaptable

Everyday a new thing happens that presents us with opportunities to learn. Engaging with a mindset that there are always new, proactive and reactive, opportunities to learn will equip you with the abilities to constantly tweak and improve all aspects of your product management skillset and knowledge.

Prepare to mess up (and learn)

Not everything you do will go to plan. When it doesn't you can sit there consoling yourself about this imperfect world or you can analyse what's happened, learn from it and move on.

Take a break

As research pooled by Harvard Business Review[15] illustrates, "keep overworking, and you'll progressively work more stupidly on tasks that are increasingly meaningless." It's ok to work hard when a particular task or initiative requires it, but continuously working around the clock only leads to burnout (and potentially a whole host of other ill effects)!

So take a break and make sure your health will support your long-term ambitions.

Effective team

Provide guidance

As a central figure in the creation and delivery of the product, it's important to provide guidance and leadership to the teams working with you. This must not be in the guise of telling them how to do their work, but providing the context that will help them focus on the right areas. As a Chief Product Officer said, "avoid being authoritarian as the team will become disenfranchised. Instead, give your teams autonomy to do their best work, but with sufficient guidance". All of which will help to create an understanding and trust that the team is working with each other's best interests front of mind.

Lead, don't micro manage

Whether its direct reports or expert collaborators, no one wants to be micro managed, it's just not motivating and doesn't bring out the best in people. Give people clear direction, stand back and watch the magic happen – you'll be surprised by the outcomes.

When describing traits of micromanaging that lead to demotivated teams, Martin Webster[16] highlights signs such as, "resist delegating work, immerse themselves in the work assigned to others, look at the detail instead of the big picture, discourage others from making decisions, and push aside the experience and knowledge of colleagues".

If you find yourself doing these, Rebecca Knight[17] suggests questions that you should ask to understand your behaviour. In summing up Rebecca's work, you can ask yourself questions such as, "is your behaviour driven by a personal insecurity? Has stepping in become the norm as a result of a period in the past when this was required? Is it being driven by pressure you feel from senior managers? Is it due to something your team has or has not done?"

If you feel you are micromanaging, it's never too late to change. Try getting feedback and letting your team tell you how they find your management style. Review yours and your team's roles with a view to clearly delineating between your work and the work of your team (especially as it may be that you are just treading into their domain). Taking on board their feedback and your role review, communicate your role and theirs and how you plan to manage going forward. Maintain an open dialogue that avoids micromanagement creeping in again.

Change is never easy, so admit that it is not going to happen overnight, but also give your team the scope to remind you when you are overstepping the mark.

Lastly, know your employees' limitations and build capabilities in the team. Your time micromanaging may have depleted some of the energy and skills in the team, or if it was because these skills did not exist you now need to build the capacity in the team so they can work effectively.

Love the expertise

Product management is about pulling a team of experts together and the more experts the better the outcome. Domain experts exist across the organisation and you need to use their valuable input to help drive your product forward.

It's important that you bring together the experts and use their insights and knowledge to support your product decisions. A passionate and friendly debate with these experts can help you get the most out of your expertise (show your passion in the debate, but ensure that you all leave shaking hands and feeling positive towards each other).

Share the decision making whilst remaining accountable

A little hard for us to get our heads around, but if we share the decision making (or at least enable our teams to influence our decisions) we will be able to use the smartness of our crowd to make better decisions.

In sharing the decision making, it does not mean passing the buck if the target outcome is not achieved. It means creating an environment where you trust and back your team to give their best answer without fearing any negative reprisals – it's called being a leader and means that (if you need to) you will happily take a hit for the long-term success of your team.

As a head of product said, "high performing product teams come together to share input". Yes, specific roles are needed but all provide their input and depending on the task, different people lead at different times. Bad product managers, take all the decisions, foist their views and alienate people.

Love your team

You're in the middle and can make people's life great or miserable. Use this wisely and they'll love you (or at least smile a lot and bring you nice edible things).

Empathise

Understand and acknowledge the feelings of another person and you take a significant step towards engaging and being able to meet their needs. Not only those of your team, the same is also for customers and stakeholders.

Empathising should not be about trying to relate to the person's situation in a disingenuous and patronising way, but ensuring that you show genuine understanding and interest.

As a people business, empathy is an important part of product management and can make or break your ability to keep the team motivated to do their best.

Develop your people

With responsibilities for people and teams, comes the opportunity to achieve more and contribute to someone else's career and development. Stretch your people, coach, guide and challenge them and let them make mistakes. Then help them pick themselves up and go at it again.

Also, see 'Section 6 Nurturing and developing your product

talent', all the suggestions there can be used with team members as much as for your personal development.

Celebrate success

You set out to achieve an outcome, so when it's achieved celebrate that success. Launching a new product is a time for a mini celebration, achieving customer acquisition numbers is a time for a bigger celebration.

Celebrating success doesn't need to mean throwing a big party, it could be much more fun and interesting. Just think if your whole team (or at least those who were interested) did a dance around the office every time you achieve an additional 10,000 or 1m customers. Sounds like fun, right? Gets the blood and endorphins pumping? Not only this, but people will want to join the team just so they can join the dancing.

Change your scenery and look in new places

It's true that familiarity leads to contempt or can at least blind us to new perspectives. To drive new thinking and views look in new places for inspiration and ideas. This can be from getting peers in other teams to comment on your product and ideas, to looking at non-competing products for ideas that you can use, challenging yourself to look at your product differently or exploring what seems like the impossible.

Move people around

When people start to do their work in system 1 mode[xi], they can start missing things. We've all been part of or heard the conversation when someone is asked about something and they

---

xi   System 1 and System 2 are two distinct modes of decision making: System
      1 is an automatic, fast and often unconscious way of thinking that is
      autonomous and efficient, requiring little energy or attention, but is prone
      to biases and systematic errors. System 2 is an effortful, slow and controlled
      way of thinking. (http://upfrontanalytics.com/market-research-system-1-
      vs-system-2-decision-making/)

give a quick off-the-cuff answer that is well versed and shows that their thoughts about it are set. Moving people around (if you can) is one way to ensure that fresh eyes and thoughts are being applied to your products. If you're the leader closely monitor the team dynamic and respond to any stagnation. Or even easier, plan to periodically move your team around to get fresh perspectives.

Bring stakeholders with you

Managing any product is a journey of trials and tribulations. To develop and sustain the relationships that are going to help you along this journey, bring stakeholders (your team, other teams, suppliers, customers etc.) with you. Ensure that they know what's going on and why and can give you input to support great decision making.

Work with stakeholders in a collaborative and transparent fashion that ensures you and your product get the right level of input and support, while your stakeholders achieve their aims. And don't forget to have empathy for them – seeing things from their perspective can be a great way to get them engaged.

Not only will this help with cohesion, it will help project the right image of product management as an inclusive and value adding function!

Effective product management

Focus on the customer

It's their prerogative to change their minds, not know what they want and be enticed by other offers – they pay the bills after all. So keep asking them what they want, keep understanding their needs and behaviours and use this to define better ways to meet their needs. And never forget that if you don't someone else will.

Every successful organisation has delivered products that customers want because they solve a problem. That is not going to change, so focus on deeply empathising with your customers, understand and obsess about their needs, and use this to deliver products that make their lives easier and better.

Be a product leader

Lead on creating and delivering a product vision, objectives/goals and strategy that meets customer needs, fits the organisation's context and focuses on returning value to the business.

Lead on being the product expert (inside and outside the organisation) who people turn to and know is focused on creating an end-to-end experience that your customers gain value from.

Lead on being the glue that brings together multiple parts of the organisation.

Lead on developing the 'we' over 'I' – a great leader knows it's a team effort and appreciates the value of recognising team contributions.

Lead by being positively influential, and using your influence to create win-win situations for you and your stakeholders.

Lead by standing up and being 'accountable' – a great leader trusts their team and is happy to devolve decision making, whilst remaining accountable for the sum total outcomes.

Focus on outcomes

100 meetings, beautiful presentations and documents, a full roadmap, pretty prototypes, etc. all account for nothing if they do not deliver outcomes that support your objectives. It is crucial to focus your efforts on the outcomes you want to achieve and ignore everything else as noise. Not an easy task as most product people will have a long list of things they would like to and could do. However, this does not mean they should be done or will add value.

As I have interviewed product people for these books, one of the things I have noticed with certain people is they focus on only a few things at a time and nothing else. Even to the point that when asked about other aspects of the role, they could not and did not want to talk about these, they just wanted to talk about the quite narrow focus they had and how this was the primary focus.

Be commercial

Meeting customer needs is crucial. Doing it at a loss will only last for so long. Even if you start with a free or low cost product, ensure you have a plan for monetisation that equates to profit: cash in the bank after you've received your revenue and paid the cost of sale. Of course, that is unless you are charged with managing a loss leader that drives engagement while other products drive profit – although even here there should be some semblance of the commercial value the product delivers.

Stay on top of the numbers

Numerical values are the easiest way to measure most outcomes, from customers to revenue to conversion rates to customer satisfaction.

Knowing what your key numbers are and focusing on driving them in the right direction is a crucial part of any product role. With big and small data, it's easy to get overawed by the different data points that are available to you, so keep your core metrics simple and use complex analysis for gaining insight and delving into a problem and gaining new insight.

Support decisions with data and insight

Use data and insight to support your decisions at every step of your product journey. Data will not provide answers to every question (it provides the what, not the why). But it does provide facts and evidence that can kick-off and drive discussion and a focus on the right areas to look at.

Signal interpreter

Learn and know how to identify and interpret signals that are telling you useful information about your customer, market, product etc. Not an easy thing to do as there is lots of noise around most industries and products. However, by creating a product radar (discussed in Product Management: Managing Existing Products) and mapping this to your vision and objectives it should be possible to continuously scan for signals.

Experiment

It is only when we try something (aka experiment) that we identify the true impact of it. They are only a test after all. A test that you can expand if it goes well, iterate or dismissed if it doesn't.

Enterprises can be risk averse places, so experiments should fit very well into a way of thinking that minimises the risk exposure and yet gives you quick ways to test and learn the art of the possible. But don't over experiment to the point of using it to abdicate thinking and decision making.

Kill ideas

There are hundreds, if not thousands, of ideas you could implement. Many of these will not fit the product or move the dial in the right direction. Be prepared to kill these ideas either before they are built or as soon as you can see they are not adding value. As Melissa Perri[18] describes, great product managers are able to eliminate bad ideas through testing them early to filter out the bad ones and speaking to the source to say, "I appreciate the feature idea you came up with, but we have tested it and we should not build it. It would be a mistake to build it. Here's why…"

Melissa also talks about the issue in most software companies being the ease at which ideas can be generated and built into features, leading to a situation where, "more often than not, we end up building most of them in hopes that something will stick." However, post release, "no one uses it."

Know your competitors

There is no point in obsessing about your competitors. However, you need to be aware that they are likely to be obsessing about your customers and looking for opportunities to take market share from you. So be clued up on their differentiators and capabilities, how they may impact your product and most importantly how you differentiate yourself from them.

Know the technology

At the centre of the digital wave is technology that enables businesses to create new products and ways of working – you need to be in the midst of this. As a minimum know what's available, the latest trends and how they can be applied as an enabler of great customer experiences. Don't stop there, go a step further by understanding and working with your team to test the future technologies that could help make stepped changes in your product offer.

You don't need to necessarily be able to code, but you do need to have an appreciation of the available and future technologies so you can identify opportunities to deliver competitive advantages and have sensible conversations with developers (right from understanding what a technology can deliver, through to appreciating the effort to implement it).

Follow the process and ignore the process

Everything is a process that takes one or more steps to complete – some processes should be static and some should be dynamic in nature. Here you need to understand the key processes that are required to get stuff done and optimise those that you can.

Some activities need a process to make them easier to manage and/or because it will always be the same each time around, while others do not need a process and should be worked out in the context.

Hygiene activities such as backlog prioritisation, delivery flow, reporting, user testing, retrospectives and planning can follow a more ridge process that is incrementally improved. While more creative work should follow processes that you define in context.

You can also link this to creating new and managing existing products. Given the nature of having nothing at the outset, new products should lend themselves to less process, while existing products should have some cadence given the many more knowns.

All processes should be up for continuous review, especially if you identify issues and/or find new and better ways of working.

Effective business alignment

Know your business

It's what the book Product Management: Business Context and Focus is all about. You need to know: what your business wants to achieve, what it sees as its priorities, what it expects from your product, and how it works and gets things done, amongst other important insights into your business.

Contribute to the culture

Today it is fair to say that the discipline of product management is one of the positive forces driving changes to how organisations operate. Product people must continue this and further promote a culture that is customer focused, open, transparent, inclusive, collaborative etc.

There are, no doubt, more things we should all do, but I think that's enough from me for now.

6

Nurturing and developing your talent

Like most careers, change is always around the corner and to remain at your best you need to learn and develop new skills on and away from your day job. Here are a number of ways to develop and nurture your career.

Know what you value the most

High on the list of activities to nurture your talent is having a clear view of what you value most (this can change over time, but at any moment in time you should know what this is). Think about what makes you tick, what you like doing, the way you want to work, the types of working relationships you want to have, the type of environment that you thrive in and the work-life balance you want to have, amongst other factors that define what's important to you.

All of these should be used to help you get the best from you, and find or create the best environment to work in (obviously not to the detriment of others).

Career plan and audit

Set yourself a 3 or 5 year career plan. Think about what you want to achieve and where you want to be. Then set a plan for how you take incremental steps to get there. Once in place, 3 or 4 times a year review your progress (what you've learned, gaps you need to fill to stay on track) and reset your plan for achieving your aims. An A4 piece of paper and a few hours is all you need. If daily life is too busy, get yourself to a coffee shop for a few hours or take it on holiday with you.

Career progression

Your next move (in line with your career plan) could be in your current organisation or elsewhere, it could be a sideways as well as a northward step. Start by looking at job specifications for the jobs you would like to do and see where your gaps are and then work on these either through opportunities in your current role, external training or reading. Within this, factor in changes in expectations of product people. A prime example is the use of data; as more data points are generated a core of any product person's role is to understand this data either through being able to crunch and analyse it, or being able to ask the right questions of the right people to gain the required insight.

Get a mentor

Find and work with an experienced and impartial person who you can openly discuss your work and career with. From brainstorming ideas, thinking of career development, getting an opinion, discussing a sensitive topic, your mentor should be a platform for discussing these and multiple other topics. If you don't already have one, go and get one.

In terms of selection, pick someone you know will be honest with you and not dumb down their words for fear of hurting your feelings. Someone you feel comfortable to talk to. Someone who has some experience in the types of organisation you work in and ideally an awareness of the roles you work in or want to work in.

Get a coach

We are constantly evolving and have (or at least should have) goals for where we want to be and/or situations that want to change. A coach will use questions and active listening to help you bridge the gap between where you are now and where you want to be. Importantly, a coach will not offer advice or give any suggestions as to what you should do. Their role is to help guide you to the answers.

Like mentoring, you can pick someone in your organisation or find an external coach – there are many professional coaches available today. So pick your goals, find a coach and start the journey to getting where you want to be.

Be a mentor

Not only does mentoring help someone else develop, it's also great for you. It enables you to develop coaching and people development skills.

Reflection and self-analysis

Often it's when things are going wrong (perceived or otherwise) that mental reviews of how we work and where we can develop and improve come about. Shift gears and make this proactive. It's good to reflect and critically analyse your own performance. Not only when times are bad, but also when times are good and you identify strengths that should be developed to further enhance your performance. This could be an exercise you run with yourself, via a friend or coach.

Practice

In the Tipping Point Malcolm Gladwell[19] says that, "in order to be an expert at something you need to practice for 10,000 hours." However, 10,000 hours may be more time than you have or need to perfect your product management skills. Instead, use each time you practice or spend time doing product activities as an opportunity to perfect your skills. Don't stop here, go a step further and set yourself some challenges and tasks.

Take an activity like customer interviews. If you need to develop your skills set an objective to complete 10 in 3 months. If you need to polish your presentation skills, set an objective of presenting to another team in the next quarter. If you need to develop customer journey mapping skills, set yourself the task of creating one for your product.

It's amazing what we can learn from our daily work. And even more amazing what we can learn when we put ourselves into new situations that require new skills. My mentor once said to me, that he did not believe so much in training courses to help people develop new skills. He preferred to give people new types of projects that will stretch them and provide real life opportunities to learn new skills.

Volunteer

If an opportunity to do something you've never done before comes up (and it's relevant to your job) or someone is short a pair of hands, volunteer to help out. It's a great way to learn new skills and try out a different role. Go a step further and if there is something your team could try that will be beneficial to you and the team, suggest it and offer to be the lead.

Personal projects

The act of doing a task is a great way to learn. However, sometimes we do not have those opportunities in our roles as the task is either taken by someone else or your current role does not require it. To acquire the skills you need, create mini-projects that will expose you to the skills you need to learn. To support your learning, set some real objectives and make it as real as possible, so in the end you will have learned by doing[xii].

---

xii   If we speak (I mean when we speak) ask me about the mini project I set-up to help me develop the skills I needed for a job role I was targeting.

Annual performance review

I have always tried to ensure that my teams' and my annual objectives covered product delivery and personal development. The latter is a particularly useful way to get your team thinking about ways to enhance their performance through learning new skills.

Product group

Not enough organisations have internal groups where like-minded people who do similar jobs can get together – even if they have 100 people in the product team. If you fancy social-sharing with your peers' set-up an internal meet-up and use this to share ideas and thoughts with those smart people you see every day.

Events

There was a day when product people did not have a space to meet and greet like-minded people. That was until groups like The Product Group and Product Tank started. The Product Group consists of 50-100 smart product people meeting and discussing product topics every month. Product Tank now has a following of thousands and c.300-400 attendees to its monthly meet-up in London alone. It also has 150+ meet-ups across the globe. If you haven't been, add this to your list of events to attend. The Product Tank organisers also put on an annual event: Mind the Product. At the London event you can expect 1,700+ attendees, excellent speakers and great networking opportunities all under one roof.

Internal activities

More and more organisations are creating internal learning channels that offer their people ways to take deep dives into new areas or short bursts of knowledge. For example, staff at Google regularly invites external speakers to address their teams. Companies like Apple, IKEA, Mars and HubSpot have their universities, and PhotoBox run lunch and learn sessions, etc. These are all great opportunities to learn new skills and knowledge to support your job and/or about other areas of the organisation.

Networking

So many of your peers have experiences and views that they are willing to share (and sometimes unburden). Get out there to networking events that focus on your product role and industry. One technique I use to gain value from networking is to go with something I want to get opinions on or test. Somehow I bring it up in conversations with fellow attendees. The responses and learnings from listening to other people's views and their challenges to my thinking have been great.

Industry knowledge

Product knowledge is great, but you should also learn about and stay up-to-date with news and information about your industry. Events, blogs, peers, Google Alerts etc. – say no more.

Reading

There are lots of great sources of information about product management out there from books to blogs to podcasts to articles. Each will have their own take from which you can learn and use to develop.

Courses

I used to look at how developers were always on another course, learning a new coding language or method. At the time I used to think wow these guys have to constantly read and update their skills – similar to medical practitioners. It is no longer just them who need to engage in continuous learning about their craft to stay at the top of their game – it's everyone, including product people. This does not just cover the practical skills such as how to conduct customer research, it includes soft skills such as communication.

Following

With many people writing and commenting on product topics, pick a few or many people you respect and like to follow. People such as Ken Norton, Marty Cagan, Jared Spool, Martin Erickson, Janna Bastow, Nir Eyal, Sean Rose, Melissa Perri, Ian McAllister, Teresa Torres, Rich Mironov etc. in the product world. And broader than this read and follow the content from notable business people, such as Eric Ries, Sheryl Sanderberg, Elon Musk, Simon Sinek, Ben Horowitz, Jake Knapp, Geoffrey Moore, Clayton Christensen, etc..

Success in your product management career will be down to being clear about what you want to achieve, equipping yourself with the right information and tools to support your success and continuously learning new skills and competencies to support your growth and development.

It is so true that no one will manage your career, except you.

Want to learn a new skill or gain a new experience? It's up to you, you need to be proactive in driving your development, so you can bear the fruits of your labours. Part of this is about identifying your learning rhythm. How do you ingest and retain new information and skills? Is it on the job? Is it through observing others? Is it by listening to a podcast on the train? Is it by discussing particular topics in a closed or open forum? Etc. Etc. You probably have more than one channel that works for you, so find them and keep using them.

7

Engaging and working with stakeholders

As mentioned repeatedly, delivering and managing a product requires a team of people and with that a team effort to complete the multitude of activities. Even more so in mid to large organisations, where product needs to engage and work with many demand and supply-side stakeholders: demand being those stakeholders that drive requirements on the product (e.g. executive), while supply-side are those who you need to call on for their input and support (e.g. customer service, legal, procurement).

Stakeholder engagement will vary depending on the maturity of the product. A major new product launch will likely require mass stakeholder engagement, while an experimental new product may require a few people to hack it together. An existing product may necessitate a smaller core group of stakeholders for less time or for ad hoc assignments. In either scenario, it's crucial to have your stakeholders fully engaged and working with you to deliver great product experiences.

Figure 12: Stakeholder Map

A great place to start is with a stakeholder map (figure 12) of the potential internal and external teams and organisations of interest.

Stakeholders can be few or many, depending on your product type and scope. The list below outlines potential stakeholders' and how they could support your product.

Stakeholder	Support they can provide
Leadership team (executives, sponsor or steering committee)	• Business context and product expectations • Setting priorities • Providing resources • Removing blockers • Providing guidance and approvals
Strategy team	• Broader business and industry direction, insight and trends

Customers	• Research and feedback
Research	• Market and customer research and proposition development
UX	• Customer research • Customer experience design incl. ensuring a consistent experience across all customer touch points
Design	• Look and feel including adherence to company brand and design guidelines
Engineering	• Product solution design incl. technical investigations • Product delivery incl. technical architecture, platform design, integrations, capacity, network infrastructure, code and platform security, development and testing, release plans, releases and in-life support
Data scientists	• Data modelling and understanding
Sales	• Direct sales • Sales toolkits and support • Friendly customer introductions for sales and research (especially in Business to Business (B2B) markets) • Create a commercial model
Commercial team and business development	• New strategic opportunity identification and development • Create partnerships and channels for distributing products

Marketing	• Proposition and messaging development • Customer communications incl. SEO, PPC, events, PR etc. • Sales toolkit • Launch plans • Internal communications
Programme and project management	• Support planning and delivering large initiatives and across teams
Customer services	• Support content • Support processes • Customer feedback • Customer survey design
Operations	• In-life support model • Incident management and resolution
Business intelligence	• Reporting • Insight
Security	• Standards and compliance
Legal and compliance	• Contracts incl. negotiation and drafting • Standards and compliance incl. data protection, privacy • Terms and conditions
Finance	• Business case incl. forecasting, costs and returns on investment • Capex (capital expenditure) and Opex (operational expenditure) requests
Partners and suppliers	• Customer research • Products, services, tools

| Logistics and operations | • Help to set-up and manage logistics and distribution |

Products will also have demands placed on them from teams or individuals. For instance, the commercial team may drive new product features, customer services may require new capabilities to deflect contacts or help them better manage customer requests, compliance may require the product to meet new regulations, branding teams may request updates to ensure compliance with brand guidelines, etc. In many ways, any or all of the stakeholders above could drive a demand as well as support the product to achieve the business and customer aims.

The more stakeholders, the harder you will need to work to keep them aligned, informed and engaged – get this right and the combined level of expertise will make for a much better product.

Enterprises are big places and it would be great if, when you joined or started work on a product, someone gave you a list of all the people you should speak to. Reality is not quite like that and I suggest latching onto someone who knows, use their network, the intranet, formal and informal meetings and people you meet to find other people you should be speaking to.

Once you understand who your stakeholders are and what is required in both directions, create a map of where they fit and how you should engage with them – remembering that although your product is a priority for you, it may not be for them.

A good way to map this is based on the influence/power and interest grid (figure 13), inspired by Mendelow's Power-Influence Grid[20].

When placing each stakeholder, selections should be based on the level of impact the stakeholder will have on your product (influence/power) and the level of engagement you require from them (interest). To help you position each stakeholder consider the following.

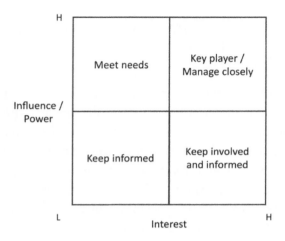

Figure 13: Influence/Power & Interest Grid

Key player/manage closely. Add people who are responsible for and will help drive decisions about the product and who therefore need to be involved in decisions and governance. Provide these people with regular updates and keep them fully engaged.

Meet needs. Add people who must be involved to get your product out the door. They hold lots of influence, however your product is not their priority, so you will need to work hard to get what you need and keep them engaged.

Keep involved and informed. Add people who are not core to delivering the product, but have a deep interest and should therefore be kept engaged and used as ambassadors. Key with these people is not to spend too much time on them, but manage their enthusiasm and engagement to the benefit of the product. If, however, their interest goes too far and they become an unhelpful distraction, then you need to directly but tactfully reduce their involvement.

Keep informed. Add people who have no interest and cannot help with your product, and should therefore be provided with general update communications.

With your list created, your next move is to engage and manage your stakeholder relationships. Whilst doing so consider the following.

Engaging stakeholders. To support your initial interactions, I suggest creating a light-touch overview. It should be concise and contextual and include background information; product objectives and the problem and solution; high level phases and timelines or a roadmap; what you require from the stakeholder, and any open questions or discussions points. Plus, anything else (without adding everything), that will help contextualise and tell your product story.

Starting stakeholder conversations. Knowing when to start conversations with stakeholders can be tricky as you don't want to waste time by arriving too early with not much to say. However, you should be thinking that, whatever the format, early engagement is key to ensuring positive engagements. I've always found that stakeholders like the fact that someone approaches them early. Many stakeholders (especially on the supply-side) also comment on not being told early enough – make sure this is not you!

In these early conversations, what you have to share with the stakeholders will depend on how far down the line you are, in terms of definition and delivery, with your product. However, the more you can share the better. I suggest not going to stakeholders with a blank piece of paper for a casual chat about your ideas and how they can help you – if you are at the early stages you should be clear about your aims, the questions you intend to answer, the plan for answering them and when and what you need from the stakeholder.

Stakeholder conversations can be exhilarating and frustrating in equal measure. You walk away from some thinking 'that was great, I'm looking forward to working together' while others will leave you wanting to bang your head against the wall. Although frustrating in these situations you should start by questioning your approach: did you explain it in language they understood? Are your aims clear? Are you speaking to the right people? And if nothing else, at least you know what the challenges are and can start to address them.

A challenge I've sometimes found is working with people whose opinions go far beyond their area of expertise and into the realms of unqualified personal opinion. Now, all input is great, but some people can go too far! Most challenging are the people who think they know everything and/or want to get involved in everything. One-to-one conversations should help with these people: have a one-to-one session with them, understand their issues and opinions and try to have an open conversation to understand where they are coming from (you'll probably learn a thing or 2 from and about them). From this you should be able to clarify their role. Sometimes this will also require politely explaining where their input is not required as other stakeholders are filling those areas (your stakeholder map will be useful here). Not always an easy task, but this is why you became a product person, right!

Stakeholder priorities. A key point when engaging and making requests is that your priority may not be theirs. This is where early engagement is crucial as it gives you a chance to identify and understand your stakeholder's other priorities and capacity to support you. Sometimes this will require a call on their time to work with you or you may need to look to alternative internal or external options – the earlier you get this in, the more time you have to go through any hoops.

Think about how you can help your stakeholder to help you. Be that through providing the information outlined above, co-working on specific pieces of work, taking them to important meetings (which saves you sharing second hand information) and generally being very open with them – when working with stakeholders on a long-term initiative, bring them into your fold and make them one of the team.

It is also a nice courtesy to provide notice of your needs early. People rightly dislike and get frustrated when they are asked for input at the last minute – especially when they could have been asked much earlier and have lots of other priorities to fulfil.

Stakeholder kick-off. After you have completed your initial round of conversations, get the relevant stakeholders in a room (or on a call) and work through the key aspects of the product with them – this should not be used to reiterate the content of the first conversation (although an overview will be useful). Instead, focus on hatching the next steps.

I know from experience that some people do not see the value of big sessions or workshops. In justifying them, it is easier to speak once, get a cross fertilisation of thoughts and opinions and use the collective knowledge of the group to shape your next steps. If, however, you don't see the value, I suggest at least staging a short conference or video call with all the relevant people to outline the product and work required to deliver. This should then be followed up by separate sessions with relevant groups.

Stakeholder accountability. To ensure engagement and motivation, a technique I've seen work very well is making stakeholders accountable for their deliverables. This may sound obvious, but how often are your stakeholders truly accountable for their deliverables as opposed to generating ideas and bringing them back to the an unqualified person (you, the product person) for approval? In this mode, the stakeholder is responsible for making decisions in their area of expertise. In terms of engagement and motivation, stakeholders should respond very well to this and really step-up and get involved.

To further motivate your stakeholders, take food and drink to sessions (it doesn't have to be pizza and beer!), offer coffees and chocolates, and most importantly ensure that the people in the room will add value.

Stakeholder negotiation. Core to stakeholder engagement is negotiation. Especially as you will not always agree on the same path – be that on a product priority or the overarching product strategy. In these situations you need to use your negotiation skills to guide you towards an agreeable outcome.

Important in this is to understand your stakeholder's perspective and drivers, and use these to discuss and debate your options until you reach a win-win that meets both of your needs. Sometimes this will not be immediately possible and you will not be in agreement. To avoid a deadlock, you may need to agree to disagree, but pick an option that you can move forward with. To help reach a decision, consider reviewing factors such as risk level or time to deliver. Once selected, whether it's yours or your stakeholder's option, you both need to agree to fully back and support it.

Not an easy thing to do, especially if the stakeholder sees it as their way or the highway. However, with discussion and debate, it should be easier to reach agreement.

Also, don't forget that part of your discussion can include looking at how you take the best parts of each option and use these to create a 3rd option (not compromise) that moves you forward. Alternatively, you could seek a 3rd option that has not yet been thought about.

External and internal stakeholder relations. External stakeholders should be treated in much the same way as internal stakeholders – especially if you want them fully engaged. You may have confidential information you cannot tell them, but withstanding this, you need to treat them as one of your team.

Stakeholder communications – At all stages of your stakeholder relationships, avoid using email and chat tools as the only means to communicate – much can be achieved in a short space of time via a face-to-face meeting or call.

Opinions, issues, challenges etc. gathered and worked through you should now know what faces you to deliver your product. Small task, big task? Few challenges, many challenges?

Ongoing, your approach to engaging stakeholders should focus on providing regular updates, sharing status and performance reports, inviting to strategy days, showcases (or 'whoo hoos' as a colleague called them) and product updates, requesting feedback etc. Not only will this help with engagement, it will also support building trust, credibility and strong relationships.

It's also important that you engage the right stakeholders at the right time and for the right amount of time. Let's say you set-up a monthly update session and invite all your stakeholders. Anyone who is invited to make up the numbers or make your product look important will eventually stop attending, while no communications or update and people may forget your product exists or that you will need their input.

When not speaking to stakeholders daily (e.g. when not working on a large initiative that requires full involvement), a good approach to maintain engagement is to communicate at least quarterly. If there is genuinely stuff to talk about, you should make this face-to-face in a session or over a coffee. Whilst if there is less to speak about, you should send an email update, highlighting things that are of interest to them.

That's it. Go collaborate and build win-win stakeholder relationships.

8

Making product management work

Mid-to-large organisations can be amazing places to work as they have the people, resources and budgets to get big things done. However, by the very nature of their size and complexity, they can also be cumbersome and slow to move. Which in turn means that being a nimble product function is harder to achieve given the potential and real blockers. With this in mind, let's explore some of the challenges and potential constraints when trying to live the product management dream, plus ways to address (or at least manage) them.

People don't understand what product people do. When asked, "what do you do?", I respond by saying, "I work in product management". This can receive either a blank response or a repeat of the question, this time only slower so as to indicate that maybe I didn't hear the first time. Alternatively, I get asked what I sell or market. Not only this, I've been called a project manager on numerous occasions – I'm still trying to work out if I've misheard the person or if that's what people think I do!

Product management in its current guise is still finding its feet in a number of organisations. As a result, many people do not know that the role exists and further do not know what it's there to do.

In time, as more people join the trade and the role becomes more familiar, this WILL decrease. For now, we just need to answer the question with a clear description of what we do, and by virtue of more people providing similar descriptions, the questions will diminish as the understanding grows.

Differing views of the product role and what it should cover. Unfortunately, by its very nature, product management can cover multiple different activities and in each organisation some of these will require product people to have deep subject matter expertise while in others a basic level will be enough, as someone else holds the expertise. A one size fits all definition of the role may never exist. However, as mentioned in the previous point, commonalities are surfacing and driving understanding, at least of the core aspects of the role. So, for now, it's our job to spread the word and reiterate, reiterate, reiterate.

Everyone does the product role (or at least a bit of it). Product people could be classed as the expert generalists that know a lot about a few things and something about many things. By breaking down the tasks a product person performs, or is involved in, you will likely find someone who is expert at many of these. Granted they may not know about other areas that relate to product management, but their skills and knowledge in that area will be more than the product folk. Take customer research, experience design, writing code, testing, data analysis etc. Each of these has specialists, whilst product people will know a bit about them.

Being an expert generalist can be a challenge if a lack of specific expertise is allowed to become a barrier. However, if product management is embraced as a role that sits in the middle, orchestrates and brings together lots of strands of activities, it starts to become the expert at joining the dots and seeing the bigger picture. Just think, if no one had that single view and everyone was going around independently doing what they thought was right, creating and delivering products would become hectic.

Roles and responsibilities are unclear. There may be overlap with another teams or departments, or the role you play may keep shifting, almost at a whim. All of which can result in product time and effort being wasted as priorities and activities chop and change, potentially without any initiative ever being concluded. Stop. Understand or define the organisational context that product operates in, map this to the role that product is to play and start clearly defining this – use the organisational fit content in Section 3 to help. Especially where there is overlap, this may require creating clear connections or dividing lines which means some responsibilities pass to product and some are removed. Which way responsibilities go should be less of a concern than clarifying the role of product, and the other teams.

Too many chefs. Whether of core strategic importance or a peripheral product, stakeholders will want to have a say and input into product decisions from propositions to features and releases. When not managed, this can create a frustrating cycle of continuously changing direction at the will of 'today's' attendees or committee. In all instances, set-up a simple way for decisions to be made and shared with all stakeholders.

To manage stakeholders' offering opinions outside your agreed decision making process, regularly invite them to the table where you can have open conversations with other key stakeholders.

If interested parties are only invited to the table intermittently or have to invite themselves, they will be out of touch with the product and only be able to offer off-the-cuff input and ideas. While those who are continuously involved and know what's happening will more likely be supporters than detractors. For instance, I once worked with a stakeholder who had little visibility of the product strategy. Every time I saw them I received questions and requests that were not aligned to the product strategy. Once this was corrected by keeping them up-to-date, involving them in relevant conversations and establishing their role, meetings became much more productive.

What's more, team autonomy and freedom to get on with the work is more probable once trust and credibility have been established.

Highest Paid Person's Opinions (HiPPOs) over facts. You are tasked with being at the heart of delivering products that customers love and in turn generate a return for the business. However, with this comes the attention of senior managers who have opinions about what you should be doing. These can resonate on the fly, during a meeting, off the back of someone having a 2-minute corridor conversation, reading an article or having a dream (seriously, this happens)! Whatever the source, it often means that with little context someone tells you that you should focus on something that does not meet a customer need or fit with the product strategy. However, because of their position in the organisation you need to take note and do what they say. The customer focused and rational answer to these requests is "no". However, that probably won't go down well.

To avoid this, set out how decisions are made and openly share that with everyone (incl. potential HiPPOs), so everyone knows what your key drivers are (e.g. decisions are driven by data and customer insight), and that they have an opportunity to input early. Then when you get that random request you have a clear response. Unfortunately, there will always be occasions when HiPPOs win over your explicit decision making processes – these are the occasions when we must just suck it up (as a colleague once said!).

No clear objectives and strategy. When in a rush to make progress, get a product out the door or when a product is in its mid-life stage, it is easy for it to run with no clear objectives or direction. To address this, stop. Well, don't down tools and completely stop work. But, take a step back and set clear objectives. This may mean setting some very short-term objectives based on things you know need to be done, while working to define the longer term objectives and direction for the product.

Although one of the mantras of lean is being agile and responsive to change, this does not negate having clear objectives and strategy.

Take an example from a peer, she worked for an organisation where no clear objectives and subsequent strategy was set for the product, this meant that the team floated along, but never really knew what they were trying to achieve – this ultimately meant that a product was c.2 years late and left this part of the organisation trailing in the market.

Revenue and profit first. Many organisations are under pressure from analysts, the city and investors to deliver year on year increases in profit, dividends and shareholder value. From a product perspective, this can lead to compromising the customer experience for a short-term financial gain.

As a head of product commented, "product management, and in particular focusing on the customer, is a long-term play. Therefore, in situations like this, it's important to find ways to integrate the customer into decisions. For instance, by conducting low cost or free customer research; surfacing customer insights to prove points and support decisions; running side-show projects and putting in a little extra-time work to capture and prove the value of customer input, and picking off small wins that incrementally raise the volume of the customer's voice."

Balancing customer and business needs is not easy. I have spoken to people who have left organisations because the battle to introduce customer focus was too hard and took too long. However, it is possible and is getting easier, as more organisations seek a better balance between the 2.

Fire fighting over seeing the bigger picture. Demand on products can run at a very high pace, which can leave the team constantly completing the next demand or firefighting instead of stopping to review outcomes and thinking about the bigger picture. Once more, stop. If the team is constantly running full steam ahead its either because it has more work to do than resources allow; the demand on the team is unrealistic; it's not well organised; no one knows how to say no or it does not have a focus and bigger picture view of what's required.

Start by understanding the cause and then make a plan for progressing towards a way of working that focuses on the most important work that links to your objectives. For instance, in one team, a separate team had to be set-up as a recurring issue kept rearing its head and meant the team spent more time on fixing a recurring problem, than working on the real value adding work.

Complex and multi-faceted product. Most products progressively grow, even in teams that deliberately cull features to stop it from becoming bloated. This can lead to a complex product with multiple parts that need to be juggled from release to release. It also means that each part of the product gets just about enough time spent on enhancing it, (which ultimately leads to mediocrity) or failure to move it forward. To address this, consider splitting the product into integrated parts that are each managed by a small team that is able to dedicate its time and efforts on making that part the best it can be. Not an easy task for products that have grown into monoliths, but it should be possible as part of a re-architecture exercise.

Legacy technology and delivery methods. Delivery of changes to big legacy systems typically require slow and methodical approaches that include 3 to 12 month release cycles. Not necessarily because that is what people want, but because the processes and systems are set-up this way and have been for many years and/or because they are creaking and the risk associated with any change is too high. Take a few quotes from engineering and test teams, "we have to test every system (even the ones that have not been changed) before we can release your product", or "I need a High Level Design (HLD) and Detailed Level Design (DLD) before I can tell you how long it will take to build", or "we can't start testing until everything has been completed and is ready", or "after I deliver my code I have to wait until tomorrow for the tester to complete their testing and raise any issues".

From a technical perspective, the simple answer may be to re-architect the platform so it's made up of interdependent but separate components – a none too trivial task. From a product perspective, it's about working with the technology team to manage the development to release cycle. Things to consider include giving the technology team the bandwidth they need to re-architect or migrate to a new platform; organising release cycles so the items released have minimal impact on the systems e.g. releasing in one area of code at a time, or iterative product releases that stack up ready for integration testing for a single combined release.

Prepare to be patient. Moving from legacy systems takes time and can be achieved in phases which means delivering value is not lost for 12 to 24 months.

Carbon copy product management. Trying to carbon copy another organisation's approach to product management. As companies hit the headlines for doing things well, it's easy for organisations to assume it's easy to take their approach and implant them, word for word, on their organisation. This is a mistake, as a product manager called out, "older companies struggle to implement product management as they are trying to shoehorn a version based on the companies they have heard are doing it well – although those companies are different".

As a central theme in all the books, it's important for individuals and organisations to create their own version of product management based on how their organisation functions. Even if another organisation's approach seems like the perfect fit, it is worth taking a step-by-step approach that enables the organisation to adjust to find its own way of working.

Demand for predictability in an unpredictable world. In many aspects of business, there is a notion that drives at predictable outcomes based on an equation of X inputs = Y outcomes. And for products that are in a certain and stable space this equation may be realisable. However, when the task is to discover something new, the challenge, as a product manager put it is to, "get people to understand that creativity is not predictable e.g. there is no straight line, it's about ups and downs with an overall upwards tick that is focused on learning over time and using the learning to hone in on opportunities that have the potential to grow exponentially".

For organisations to overcome this, they need to either invest in bets[xiii] (Alphabet-style) or start looking early, before the organisation is in need of the golden egg – especially as those who typically wait, end up losing out on opportunities (and even folding). As the same product manager said, "this approach needs to also run outside of budget cycles that typically tie searches and returns to a specific window of time rather than leaving them free to explore the art of the possible".

Lack of resources. Whether grand aspirations are held for the product or just a few small requirements, most of the time there is a lack of resources and a feeling that if this was addressed more value could be delivered. However, a bottomless pit of resources does not exist and doing more with less is the order of most days.

---

xiii   Investment in initiatives that you do not know if they will succeed or not, but are willing to take a chance on the basis that they have the potential to pay off.

It is unlikely that doing everything will ever be possible. The challenge is to work out what realistic resources are required to achieve your objectives, and plan for these. Whether the needs are people, budgets, tools, equipment etc., these need to be mapped to outcomes that apply rational justification and prioritisation.

Organisational complexity. Large organisations can be complex places with multiple interlinked nodes of capabilities that move at different paces, but must work together to support your products (figure 14).

Take all the stakeholders and departments (e.g. customer service, technology, legal, operations, marketing, finance etc.) that have a role to play in the end-to-end customer experience. It can be a daunting task to keep these aligned and singing from the same hymn sheet.

To address this, start by using stakeholder maps to work out who you need to work with and plan for how you manage each relationship. Also (I'll say it again), start work early to understand how each stakeholder works, their priorities and pressures so you can work with them towards a win-win.

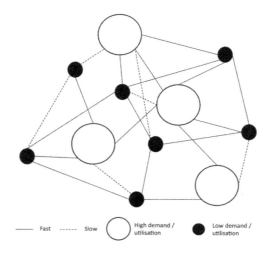

Figure 14: Flow of Work and Utilisation of Business Capabilities

Silos. Teams and people operate closed systems that keep everyone on the outside, so they retain complete control and shine a light on how good they are over others. Sadly, this is human nature (for some)! To address this, start by demonstrating that you work in an open, transparent and collaborative way – emphasising and illustrating the benefits through your actions rather than words. Once you demonstrate this behaviour, the team will see it and be more likely to engage.

Protectionism. Historical organisational structures and ways of working can make the simplest task seem complex and time consuming. Because it has worked for many years and/or because its only just been made to work, some organisations and departments are not prepared to change or find many reasons why change is not required. A case in point: when speaking to a project manager about using an Agile approach to deliver a new platform, he vehemently responding by saying that while he was in the company he would not deliver iteratively due to the risk it presented.

Unfortunately, in a number of organisations, this is going to be the frustrating stance for a while (of course, not negating the fact that there may be other factors at play!). Be patient and try to become the catalyst for change. Vested and personal interest usually sit at the heart of protectionism – usually driven by a fear of change[xiv] and/or a need to protect hours of effort invested in getting to the current state.

To address this, bring the people along the journey so they become invested in making the necessary changes. Techniques

---

xiv Andrea Simon, Ph.D. cites 3 reasons why humans fear change: (1) habits are powerful and efficient. (2) the brain hates change. (3) people have to see and feel new ways of doing things, not just read about them. Andrea also defines ways to address this fear: (1) get out of the office. (2) go exploring. (3) build an innovation culture. (Andrea Simon, Ph.D., "Why We're So Afraid of Change – And Why That Holds Businesses Back", Forbes, 8th April 2013, www.forbes.com/sites/womensmedia/2013/04/08/why-were-so-afraid-of-change-and-why-that-holds-businesses-back) include understanding why they work the way they do, explaining why there is a need to work differently and using this as the launch pad for finding common ground and a shared new way of working that meets both party's needs.

Bureaucracy. What started off as good governance and light-touch processes to support the business operations take over and slow down your product plans. Take a product approval process in a financial institute, this required hours just to understand the process, then more hours to fill in forms at each step, followed by the formal sign-off committee – all just to start an initial round of research!

First, although this can feel like a burden, not all processes are unnecessary. Aim to get ahead of the game to understand why the processes are there and how to manage them effectively. Second, most processes have an owner. If you can embed them in the team, so they get answers to their questions first-hand without requiring you to pour over forms for hours. Lastly, consider making a recommendation for changes that could loosen the reins by separating high impact governance requirements from low risk activities. And even go as far as recommending or at least implementing, in your own area, a beat the b*llsh*t squad – culture dependant, of course!

Politics. Jostling for position and working to personal or departmental agendas is ingrained in most organisations – especially when everyone has to scrap for budgets and priority calls, as subconsciously we all know that everyone's plans cannot be achieved.

Politics, in these situations, are not easy to address. Unless you have an organisational culture that fights against it, by for example focusing everyone on what is best for the customer and company over personal or departmental agendas. If the culture supports eliminating politics, being open is the best way to operate. If it does not then you've just got to work hard to stay focused on achieving your objectives and tackle each political obstacle as it arrives (sad, but true).

Nothing happens overnight, it takes time to change years of ingrained thought processes and ways of working. Start somewhere and play an incremental game that is about bringing people along with you on a journey one step at a time.

9

Future of product management (is now)

Industries and organisations continue to evolve and change. Product management is no different and over the coming years it will shift in its own right and through drivers that emanate from other sources.

So, what lies around the corner for product people? How will the role change in the years ahead? What will product people need to do to be successful? Here are a few thoughts on the future of product management.

Future 1: Customer, customer, customer

Customer focus is already a mantra for product management and will become even stronger over time. Product roles will become even more laser focused on the customers' needs and be a pillar of understanding customers and using this insight to drive the organisation forward.

CxO[xv] priority initiatives around the customer and customer experience coupled with the product emphasis on the customer furthers the potential for product (as well as UX) roles to lead in this space.

Future 2: Analog meets digital and creates new product people

A new kind of product person is required to work in a world where traditional and digital ways of doing business co-exist.

Digital was once a cottage industry overshadowed by traditional products that generated the revenue. As a result, digital people and their products sat on the periphery. As the internet has grown, digital products have expanded to compliment or replace more traditional products. Not only this, but digital products have been able to capitalise on the internet being bits and bytes and therefore more easily updated than traditional products.

This and advances in delivery methods has led to the rise of a new type of product manager who is heavily focused on products that utilise digital technologies. Traditional means of delivery have not gone away but are now working alongside or being merged into these new ways of working. In a reverse of the move that has been played out for many years, the online to offline world[xvi] is growing and reinforcing the co-existence of the 2 as more equal partners.

The journey is only part way through and as progress is made the merging of the 2 is required to operate in this new world (figure 15).

To achieve this new way of working, both need to combine their know-how and in doing so create new product people who understand and are able to work in both environments.

---

xv   CxO refers to senior executive level officers in the organisation e.g. Chief Executive Officer, Chief Product Officer, Chief Technology Officer, Chief Marketing Officer etc.

xvi A world in which online and offline channels share the same importance in an organisation's strategy for achieving success.

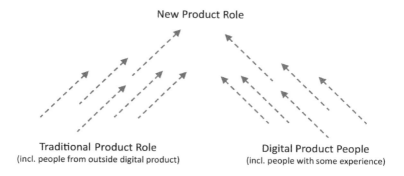

Figure 15: From Traditional vs Digital Product Management to a New Product Management World

While organisations work through this shift there will be rounds of trial and error – some of which will see speedy transformations while others will lead to frustration for individuals and teams. A sure sign of progress will be when the word 'digital' is taken out of the vocabulary and everyone just talks about product!

Future 3: Collaborate or get out the way

Looking at the broader organisation, there is a strong movement towards increased collaboration across teams and disciplines.

Today, the term collaboration is spoken about a lot, but in reality is not lived by most teams. If you meet with someone regularly and tell them what you're doing and ask them to do 'stuff' that isn't collaboration. Real collaboration means sharing and working towards the same goal; seeking and taking input from everyone who is involved; when in the moment removing all hierarchical structures and working on an equal basis; acting as one regardless of function and departmental boundaries; etc. A bit like a great football team[xvii]. They enter the field as one, move forward and back together, and if someone finds themselves out of

---

xvii If not a football fan, please substitute for your team sport or activity of choice.

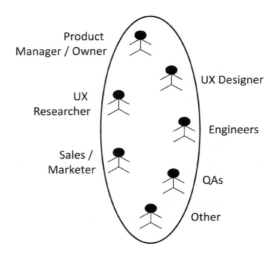

Figure 16: Spotify-type Squad

position a team member slots in to cover. Each person has a role to play and appreciates the importance of each other, and the fact that as one cohesive unit their chances of success are much higher.

Organisations are trying to replace silos[xviii] and create bridges with cross-functional working and communal spaces where all disciplines work together. An example of this is Spotify's Squads[21] that brings together multiple disciplines to work in cross-functional teams (figure 16).

For instance, at a gift company, multiple squads (including a product manager, engineers, design, and marketing) have been created around Pirate Metrics[xix] – each has a Pirate Metric. In addition, there are squads that look after the product platforms and capacity. A central roadmap exists so all teams know what each other

---

xviii Departments or groups unwilling or unable to share knowledge.

xix Describes an easy to remember acronym (AARRR) that cover many of the metrics that drive the success of a product or business. A = Acquisition, A = Activation, R = Retention, R = Referral & R = Revenue. (Dave McClure, Startup Metrics for Pirates: AARRR!, Master of 500 Hats, 6th September 2007, http://500hats.typepad.com/500blogs/2007/09/startup-metrics.html)

are working on and can work together on specific themes and/or even avoid clashing in specific areas: whether that's around creating a clear runway for experiments or working on the same code in parallel.

Successful product delivery requires cross-functional working and therefore finding ways to collaborate is the order of the day. As a study of executives[22] found, "profitability increases when workers are persuaded to collaborate more" … "If a company wants to outstrip its competitors, it needs to influence not only how people work but also how they work together".

Future 4: Business leadership roles

Product in digital environments (and maybe beyond) is well positioned to take on a heartbeat position in organisations. To truly take on that role, product people will need to further develop skills, knowledge and understanding across business areas such as business strategy, finance, operations and all the other General Manager-type responsibilities. Not necessarily at the level of being able to do those jobs, but to understand and be able to have great conversations and influence the respective leaders in those areas.

Many product people already think this way, and product is gaining traction at the c-suite[xx]. For instance, product has board representation at Facebook and Google. Further CEOs are being sourced from the product ranks in companies like Microsoft (Satya Nadella), Google (Sundar Pichai), Yahoo (Marissa Mayer) and PepsiCo (Indra Nooyi). Going even further, organisations, such as Twitter, Dropbox, Facebook, Google, etc. offer product leadership programmes[23] with an aim of creating the business leaders of the future.

The challenge is now to deliver a repeatable model that sees people, with backgrounds in product, lead across multiple organisations and industries.

---

xx   Term used to collectively refer to corporations most senior executives.

Future 5: A product person for many products

Traverse the web and you will find a multitude of job adverts that seek people to manage a particular product.

Today, many job specifications are written to cover specific roles. And even then, by the very nature of writing a specification for a particular product, the recruiter is held down to thinking about that role and only that role.

What's even crazier is that it's counterintuitive to the needs of the person and organisation. Most employees would love to know that they will have a varied career (in the same organisation, if possible) that includes easily moving around to work on lots of products – and these specifications don't deliver against that!

As an alternative, there is a company (or 2) who think a little differently and proactively look for product people who can ply their trade across a range of products, be that mobile, web, bots[xxi], B2C (Business to Consumer), B2B (Business to Business), platforms, internal applications etc. A summary of a Deliveroo job description[24] exemplifies this (box 1).

Box 1: Summary of Deliveroo Product Management Job Description

---

- At Deliveroo Product Management "takes many forms, and involves many facets". These facets include working on customer facing websites and apps, apps to direct a fleet of drivers across the globe, delivering services and ways of interacting to partner restaurants and delivering and managing internal tools for teams such as customer service and finance, amongst others.
- A Deliveroo product manager role can mean "working on any or all of these areas" and tackling "new problems, address[ing] new challenges, and find[ing] new, creative ways to apply yourself to the problems at hand."

---

xxi Software application that runs automated tasks over the internet.

This is great for a few reasons: 1, it shows that there is scope to move around and enjoy a long and varied career in the organisation. 2, it shows that the organisation has a flexible approach and moves their people around to focus on the priorities. 3, it sounds like an awesome career pathway.

Future 6: Ubiquitous presence

Product management is almost everywhere. Over the next few years' product management will not only reach into most or every organisation, it should (hopefully will) also start to establish common descriptions of its purpose. When colleagues can describe the product role and the value it brings to the organisation that will be the day this has been achieved.

In a conversation with a business analyst, they asked about what product people do, to which I replied with a brief description. Instantly, they responded that their organisation could do with a product person to drive their products forward as no one had an overarching view of the product direction and was responsible for pulling together the various strands to ensure it was delivering. At best what they had was a project manager who tried to filter and direct requests, but that was it. Hearing that made me smile.

Product people, we have an important role to play – we just need to tell more people about what we do and (of course) demonstrate our value!

Future 7: More technology and user experience

Product people will need to ensure they have the right level of technical and user experience, knowledge and understanding. For many roles, these will be pre-requisites. Or as a minimum, those who have them will have an advantage over other candidates.

On the technical side, although I do not have an engineering background, I have always found it useful to understand technological capabilities and be able to use this when speaking to developers. As a product manager once said, "knowing the technology creates a shared understanding with developers, which in turn makes it easier to work closely. It also makes it easier to spot the b*llsh*t (no offence intended developers, it works the other way too) and empathise with the challenges."

On the user experience side, I once worked with a team of product people who had basic coding and practical user experience skills. Having both of these enabled them to quickly create basic prototypes for testing new product ideas – it was magic and sped-up the process.

In both instances, this does not mean product people will do the job of developers or UX designers. Quite the opposite, the need for both roles is expanding rapidly and the product side is more about being able to hold informed conversations, while the skills and expertise of professional developers and UX people focus on the specialist tasks.

Future 8: Learning, not failing

Today, much is said about learning through failure as a way of working. However, many organisations do everything they can to avoid failing. So much so that progress is slowed while trying to find the perfect answer that eliminates any chance of failure. Dan Levin, COO of Box[25] put it perfectly when he said that, "people in large companies slow down because they are afraid of being wrong (failing)".

I remember working in an organisation that claimed to have a test and learn culture, however so much emphasis was placed on getting it right by not doing the wrong thing that it was hard to feel that something not working could be a learning opportunity. Not only this, but post-test there was no conversation about what had been learned and how the learning could be used to achieve a positive outcome going forward.

Moving away from a fear of failure is a cultural shift that requires a commitment to not only running experiments, but ensuring that lessons are captured and used when failure occurs. If learning from failure is encouraged, the value of continuously testing becomes clear and conversations about not running tests because the last one did not work eliminate themselves.

As Tom Chi[26], said, "don't fail fast, learn fast". Organisations will move towards a mode that focuses on the learning and not the failure, in that it is after the event that the learning becomes important.

Future 9: Unleashing innovation through eliminating personal risk

To push more products or experiments into market, encourage innovation, exploration and risk-taking, some organisations are working with what I call incremental product strategies.

These provide funding and time blocks for new product ideas to incrementally prove their value before being given the go-ahead to continue. For instance, as a first step the organisation may commit a set of resources to understand the market. Once insights have been reviewed, it will then make a continue/can decision.

As good as this sounds, where teams are used to being given the go-ahead to deliver over a long period of time, this can be unsettling. Especially as most organisations train employees to think in terms that equate product failure to job losses.

Organisations seeking to address this fear can make 'test and learn' a standard that includes opportunities for the learners to use their experiences on other product ideas.

Tied to this is the idea that organisations start work on future product initiatives in advance, so they are ready before the old one runs out of steam.

Modelling this you might have overlapping Product Life Cycles (PLC), so as a product grows (and before it reaches peak

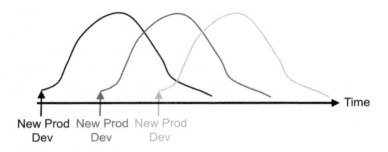

Figure 17: Overlapping PLC

performance), work starts on the next version (figure 17). As an executive who was working on such a product strategy once said: 'it's better to eat our own lunch than have someone else eat it'.

More organisations are taking a version of this approach and setting up new or empowering existing product teams to create fledgling products. Using a tool such as Plan/Go/Stop (more on this later) will help manage this process.

Future 10: On the fly and embedded innovation

Although innovation labs[xxii] have been around for a while and are used to explore and test new ideas and technologies, more teams and organisations will deliver innovation on the fly. In fact, organisations such as Microsoft, Disney, Turner Media, New York Times[27] have closed their innovation labs – some have moved the responsibility and investment into the core teams.

Innovation will be ingrained in day-to-day product delivery as a way to deliver stepped and incremental improvements to

---

xxii A typical cycle for an innovation lab might be to generate ideas (with no knowledge of feasibility), then review each based on costs, feasibility, time to market, etc., then kill off one by one until there are one or a few ideas that can be reviewed in detail and/or delivered. From here scoping and delivery starts.

products. Take a team that is developing new product features, rather than just looking to the technologies they have always used, they will look broader and seek the best and most current technologies for the job at hand. They will also proactively be looking for innovation they can apply to improve their products.

Where innovation labs exist, they will be more closely aligned to the products and functions they are seeking to help innovate. For instance, a company I worked for had an innovation team that was separate from the core business (they even had a special pass to get into their area). This team had the latest tech and worked on some cool stuff. However, their work was separate to the core business and typically no one found out about what they were doing until it was complete. Great if you want to play around with the latest this and that. Not great if what they are working on bears little relevance to the core customer problems that the product teams work on and would love to innovate around. This lab was eventually shut down and the budget and teams moved to work alongside the products they were trying to help.

Future 11: College and university education

Most people who enter product management enter via an adjacent career such as marketing, sales, business analysis, engineering, user experience, customer research and strategy. Which is great as it means those people bring to the role an understanding of one or more areas that are core to product management.

Today, there are many courses provided by organisations such as Mind The Product Training, General Assembly and Product School. Going forward, as the discipline further evolves, there will likely be more college and university courses on the subject, so people can make this a career choice from the outset.

Future 12: AI, Bots, IoT, AR and VR

AI, Bots, AR and VR have the potential to (will) completely change the product landscape and in particular the inner workings of the way customers interact with products.

Artificial Intelligence (AI) and Bots. Bots could reduce the number of interfaces and how users interact with products by reducing some of the complexity and friction. For instance, rather than 4 or 5 apps to organise my night out, a single bot could manage the whole experience including linking and sequencing activities and managing a pre-defined budget[xxiii].

Augmented Reality (AR) & Virtual Reality (VR). By creating environments that mix reality with virtual worlds (AR) and/ or creating or replicating real world experiences, the options for products grows significantly. Take buying furniture, no more does the customer pick up an app, browse the range and imagine the furniture in their home. No, they either overlay the item on a view of their room or quickly create a likeness of their home and add the furniture to it. So the first time they get a feel for how the furniture fits in their home is not when they get it home.

Internet of Things (IoT). Increased merging of software and hardware will create truly intelligent cities, offices, and homes that act on your behalf and provide you with services and information.

There's a whole new world of opportunities that have started or are coming very soon. And let's not forget areas such as creating products that work in autonomous cars! To prepare for these and the many other futures that will come the way of product management and business in general, the best advice is to be curious and learn. Product management is a dynamic profession

---

xxiii I've drafted a draft blog on this topic, maybe once you're reading this book I will have published it!

and only by listening, reading, talking and searching for the next future will we all continue to evolve and stay relevant.

So there you have it. Some insights into the role and what it takes to master.

Before finishing, in the next section I'd like to introduce a few tools that you may find useful: the Product Scroll and Plan, Go, Stop.

10

Tools to help get the job done

Tools, models, constructs, applications etc. Product management is fortunate enough to have many to support the community. Here we'll add to this with a tool for capturing the overarching product story (the 'Product Scroll') and an approach for incrementally planning and delivering your product activities (using 'Plan, Go, Stop').

Product Scroll

Every product needs a story that will help to focus and bring the people working on it together. The 'Product Scroll' is a tool for achieving this. It helps to define and set out the core elements of your product offer when you are bringing it to market and in-life (figure 18).

Why a scroll you might ask! Well, no 2 product stories are the same and although this needs to be kept high level, typically some areas require more explaining and detail than others and the scroll allows you to achieve this.

Figure 18: Product Scroll

Going back in history, a message would literally be announced as it was 'rolled out'. I'm not saying you need to go as far as rolling up your product story (although it would be fun), but you are telling a story in much the same way and need to have the ability to elaborate or keep it short, as required.

Although covered in detail in books **Product Management: Bringing New Products to Market** and **Product Management: Managing Existing Products**, we can at least highlight some of the questions you will seek to answer as you create and manage your Product Scroll:

- **Business context and focus:** what is the business direction and its priorities and what is the required/expected contribution from product management?
- **Product Vision:** what is your aspiration for the product?
- **Goals, Objectives & KPIs:** what does your product need to

achieve/contribute to the business and customers, ⸺ will success/the journey towards success be measured?

- **Product strategy:** what is the customer problem statement (job, customer segments, alternative options, market insights) and solution (product experience, priorities etc.) to address it?
- **Product strategy execution:** how will you identify the problem statement and then create the product to address it?
- **Product support:** which accompanying activities (pitch/ business case, budgets, price, sales & distribution, partnering, legal, customer communications, customer support, internal comms etc.) need to be completed and who or how will they be completed?
- **Appendices:** what information is needed/do you have to support the product?

The life of a Product Scroll starts when you initiate your product and is updated as you go through your phases of development and management. As a scroll with headings it also helps you identify the areas you need to focus on and the associated priority – which leads nicely to the next tool: Plan, Go, Stop.

Plan, Go, Stop

When creating a new product or delivering a major enhancement to an existing product, you should work in increments of activities that are ideally time boxed and allow you to incrementally and continuously learn. To support this, you can use the Plan, Go, Stop tool which is designed to help you manage incremental product delivery.

Plan, Go, Stop drives action and uses checkpoints to review progress and decide on your next actions. Plan is about creating a set of activities with measurements in a given period of time. Go is about completing those activities. At the end of the Go period, Stop kicks in as a means to review and evaluate the outcomes before you decide on your next step (figure 19).

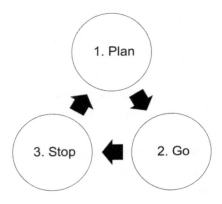

Figure 19: Plan, Go, Stop

Plan

At the start of your strategy creation and execution process you need a plan. Not a detailed plan that takes weeks to create and is out of date the day its agreed, but one that gets you going, can be adapted and helps reduce risks as you learn.

Sound good?

Ok, let's bring this to life with the 'Pen/Pencil Plan' (or P/PP for short). The P/PP allows you to spend a little time thinking about all the things you need to and could do to deliver your product into market. It then only prescribes that you create a detailed 'pen' view of the first phase of activities. Other activities can be sketched into a skeleton 'pencil' plan or task list of follow-on activities (box 2).

Box 2: Pen & Pencil definitions

Pen = concrete actions to do now

Pencil = open actions that can change at the end of each phase/step (e.g. add or remove a future activity esp. if this phase answered questions that you had for later)

This approach enables you to specify and deliver small chunks of work, after which you review the outcomes and learnings and decide on your next steps.

First up, create a list of the key activities you think need to be completed e.g. desk research, customer interviews, ideation, mock-ups etc. Divide this into 2 lists: 1 to be worked on now and 1 to be worked on later.

At this stage more of your time should be spent listing the 1st set of activities. However, you should spend a brief period thinking about the 2nd list – as this is your early opportunity to highlight any crucial unknowns, risks, blockers and constraints (e.g. resource availability, budget, dependencies, other priorities, technology dev/lead-cycles) that you should start thinking about now. Importantly, in mid to large organisation (where dependencies are rife) I would not suggest leaving conversations in these areas until too late as that may leave you with blockers that could have been avoided.

Sketching out the activities is also useful to drive your decision making and help manage your own (and others) expectations about the process (and timelines).

With all of this in mind, a first cut P/PP for launching a new product could look 'scrappy' (figure 20) or more formal (figure 21).

One of the criticisms of techniques such as Agile, in large organisations, is that you never know when stuff is going to be delivered and therefore no one knows what it will cost and if it will meet a business deadline e.g. launch before the summer or Christmas period. Creating a skeleton plan seeks to address some of that by providing a sketched timeline to complete your activities, with scope within that to change your approach as you learn.

Before you start work on a P/PP it's crucial that you and the people you will share the plan with know and buy into the approach. The creation of your initial plan and subsequent reviews and re-alignments should involve the core team who will be

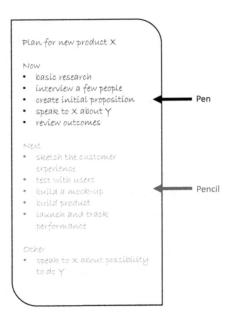

Figure 20: Scrappy Plan

working on the tasks e.g. design, UX, dev etc. To ensure support and engagement, I suggest being transparent by pinning your approach/skeleton plan to a wall or board, where everyone can see it. If printing stuff out is not an option (remote teams and all that), you should make them available in a shared workspace where everyone can see and use them.

Getting your core team and stakeholders involved in creating the plan, having rationale discussions about what's important to focus on and sharing the plan ensures that your plans are matched by the skills and resources available in your organisation. It is also a great way to engage the people who are central to your success through generating the buy-in and support you require.

	Activity	Target outcome
Plan, Go, Stop 1 (2 weeks)	• Create product hypothesis/ guesses/ assumptions • Gather desk research (market and customer) to validate/disprove the hypothesis • Interview prospective customer segments	Clear problem definition and initial segment identified
Plan, Go, Stop 2 (2 weeks)	• Create product proposition and test with prospective customers • Investigate development and support/operations options	
Plan, Go, Stop 3	• Create product concepts in a storyboard and test with customers • Update hypothesis, product proposition and storyboard • Create business case	
Plan, Go, Stop 4	• Build a clickable prototype and test with customers • Update hypothesis, product proposition and storyboard	
Plan, Go, Stop 5	• Build product and go live • Set-up dedicated early market operations capabilities and team • Gather data and insights	
Plan, Go, Stop 6	• Implement growth campaign • Start work on new features • Track metrics	

Figure 21: Formal Plan

Not only this, but it does help to ensure that everyone's areas of interest are represented. I remember having just such a conversation with a former colleague. At the time they were trying to agree on a support model for their, yet to be launched, product. This meant they had the contact centre planner requesting long-term acquisition and retention numbers (so they could allocate the right level of resources) even though they did not have these. After a brief discussion we agreed that it was important to understand why they needed the long-term numbers and how they did their planning (e.g. was it based on the time it took to stand up the team). Pre-empting the answers, we thought that a good approach would be to provide figures for time blocks that allowed them to plan and recruit (if required). Following a conversation, they reached agreement to provide numbers that covered time blocks which gave them time to plan their resources.

When creating your P/PP it's important to communicate that only the first phase is hard wired. This is very important for your stakeholders and you as you do not want your skeleton plan to become a hard wired list of activities and timelines – your learnings will be used to adjust your activities.

While thinking of the activities to support the P/PP approach, there are 2 primary things to avoid.

Having no plan. I have and I've seen others, get straight into the doing and not spend any time thinking and planning what they are going to do and why – the result of which has been a set of disconnected activities, activities that go on for longer than necessary, wasted time as activities that could have been done in parallel are completed concurrently, resources not being available when required and poor expectation management.

Lacking urgency. I once worked in a group where there was no sense of urgency or drive to get stuff done. This meant that after each phase of work, we went back to the drawing board and either realised that we could have covered some of it in the previous phase, repeated some of the work or tried to book unavailable resources – had we been more planned in our approach… Lesson learned!

As I think of the products I have worked on, and in particular the ones that have gone very well, I have always set out with some kind of plan or view of the phases of work and along the way I have made changes to accommodate new information and discoveries. Those plans have also helped me be clear about what I need from each phase (and my stakeholders).

Not only does this approach help you get going now, whilst also thinking ahead about what will be required to complete product development. It also helps you focus on the next most important activities; creates checkpoints unique to your product and context; stops product delivery timelines from floating along, and demonstrates that you have balanced having a clear direction with flexibility to use learnings as you progress.

In terms of end-to-end timeframes, you need to factor in considerations such as where are you today and what is required to achieve the end goal e.g. if you know nothing about the market, you may need more time to get up to speed; when does your business want the product to launch and is this driven by immovable dates e.g. is it tied to a particular season or date and is there a window of opportunity.

Go

Do what it say's on the tin, and get going executing your plan for this phase until you complete the activities or your time runs down.

During the Go phase you should refer to your plan for guidance, but not feel restricted from altering it to meet your target outcomes. This includes moving to the Stop phase early if you finish and calling a stop if you need to redress your plan and take a different approach.

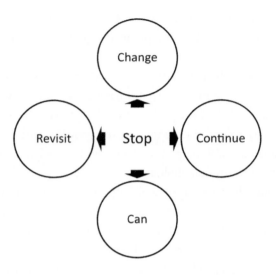

Figure 22: Stop & Decide Options

Stop

Once you get to the Stop point, you are ready to review the outcomes and decide on your next steps. Here you have 4 options: continue, change direction, revisit or cancel the product initiative (figure 22).

In reviewing where you are, you should seek to swap assumptions with evidence and facts, using these to help make your decisions.

If the outcomes are positive and show progress, you will likely decide to '**Continue**'. Continuing will mean taking the learnings from the previous step and using them to set the next stage of activities.

If the outputs from the previous phase were inconclusive or raised a number of areas for further work (or if you ran out of time to complete them) you may want to '**Revisit**' or continue working on the phase so you can reach a clear decision.

It's important that you only take the decision to '**Revisit**' if you have unknowns or open questions that either block you from going forward and/or will have a material impact on the decision you make. If it is just that you would like more time to make perfect your information, then you should make a decision with what you have and move forward.

If your outcomes showed a major assumption to be incorrect, identified an opportunity that you did not think of, highlighted that a different customer segment had the need, that the job is different or that you were focusing on the wrong platform etc., then you may want to 'Change Direction'[xxiv].

You may want to 'Cancel' the product initiative or place it on the backburner if the outcomes indicate that there is no problem, it is not important to potential customers, the market is very niche and has little potential for growth, there are external blockers beyond your control (e.g. changes in the law), the solution would be impossible (given current technical capabilities) or take too long and cost too much to deliver.

On exercising the option to cancel, this can be great in principle, however the reality of being able to cancel or even suggest that a product initiative is cancelled will be down to company culture and how it views the development cycle. Is saying cancel a career affecting failure or is it applauded for saving the business time, money and resources!

Organisations that promote discovery mode as opposed to Just F***ing Do It (JFDI) are more likely to be comfortable with the cancel option. While if it's a space they see as crucial for their success, they will at least entertain the options of changing direction or revisiting the initial direction.

Compared with more traditional ways of working, this requires a different mentality and organisational culture that is

---

xxiv Typically companies pivot, while products change direction. Pivots are business strategy-led, changing direction is product strategy-led – Apple, HP, Lego, Nintendo, Nokia, Netflix, Google etc. are established companies that pivoted. Adobe, and Microsoft changed direction when moving to the cloud.

focused on continually learning and using those learnings to make decisions, whatever that decision will be. More about the 'open' organisational culture that is likely to promote this way of working can be found in the book **Product Management: Business Context and Focus**.

I successfully used the Plan, Go, Stop approach on a product initiative in a bank. Here I had an overall view of the phases of work to get the product into market. But rather than create a lengthy plan containing details of each phase of work, I focused on the next set of actions and gave them a time window of anything from 2 weeks to 2 months. At the end of each phase, the outcomes were reviewed and decisions taken on the next steps.

Plan, Go, Stop is about guiding your ways of working, not creating rigid structures. It is designed to be a flexible enabler of learning and adjustments as you go through the process of delivering your products.

Mid to large organisations can be complex places. So a little time spent thinking about and setting out your plan then reviewing it at appropriate times could save a lot of time later and provide an early view of the real effort to deliver your product.

There are many routes to deliver your product to market and the Plan, Go, Stop should help you pick off bite sized pieces of work that you can time box and complete before you take the next step. You should not set unrealistic time boxes that you know will lead to the wrong decision and/or not give you enough time to get the right answer. However, you should be thinking along the lines of activities that take between 1 to 4 weeks to complete – this will help to keep you focused and avoids having ideas or activities that go on and on.

Plan, Go, Stop is designed to be flexible and easy to use in any organisation. In summing it up, there are a few principles I suggest you use as guidance.

Don't wait for the perfect strategy or plan. It will never happen. You need to understand and define what is important before you start and what you can learn as you go through your journey. In the past, many businesses would not do anything without completing a detailed study of the opportunity – and then once they got into market they'd find out that the data they gathered 12 to 18 months ago had changed and was outdated.

Make working in increments your mantra. You will always be learning, learn in increments that can be applied to your product. Small chunks of work that can be reviewed will mean that you can move fast, learn fast and use your learnings in near-real-time. It also means you can quickly adjust your approach without having gone too far in the wrong direction.

'Can it' if it's not going anywhere. Don't try and force something on your customers if they don't want it and/or the solution is impossible or not cost effective to deliver. A few knockbacks are fine, but if you get to the point where the customer is saying no to every approach you take, give up on that idea completely or go back to basics and rethink your product.

That's it

I've shared all I have to share… for now!

I hope you have found this book useful. Whether an experienced product manager or new to the discipline, I hope the experiences and descriptions in this book help you to optimise your role and how you get product management done.

This series of 4 books (including **Product Management: Understanding Business Context and Focus, Product Management: Bringing New Products to Market and Product Management: Managing Existing Products**) contains many founding principles for product management, but these are just the beginning and your experiences and thoughts should drive you to develop and adapt these to create new ways of working.

Try new things, work out how your organisation works and feed through your ideas in a way that works for them, and you.

If you find a way and your words fall on positive ears, great. But if they don't, try another angle and persist. In the past 5-10 years, many organisations have started investing in product management and many of its core principles, so keep going and don't give up.

Just before I go, I must thank Donna Rawlings for conscientiously copy-editing and providing constructive feedback and advice on the flow and structure of the 4 books.

I've really enjoyed the journey in writing this book and sharing my product management story. If you have a story to tell and/ or an alternative view to those in this book, please share those at www.asomiithia.com or www.productmanagementseries.com.

Asomi Ithia

References

1. p 83, The HP Way, David Packard, Collins Business Essentials, 1995
2. Dharmesh Shah, "The HubSpot Culture Code: Creating a Company We Love", HubSpot Blog, 10th July 2018, https://blog.hubspot.com/blog/tabid/6307/bid/34234/The-HubSpot-Culture-Code-Creating-a-Company-We-Love.aspx
3. Richard Banfield, "The Importance of Product Vision to Product Leaders", 17th January 2017, https://medium.com/@freshtilledsoil/the-importance-of-product-vision-to-product-leaders-c33ecc2b9b96
4. Facebook, https://en-gb.facebook.com/careers/teams/product-management
5. Chandra Gnanasambandam, Martin Harrysson, Shivam Srivastava, and Yun Wu, "Product managers for the digital world", McKinsey & Company, May 2017, www.mckinsey.com/industries/high-tech/our-insights/product-managers-for-the-digital-world
6. "Product Management Insights", Alpha 2017 Insights, http://insights.alphahq.com/hubfs/Content/2017%20PM%20Insights.pdf
7. "What is a day in the life of a product manager at Google, Facebook or Yahoo like?", Quora, 4th October 2015, www.quora.com/What-is-a-day-in-the-life-of-a-Product-Manager-at-Google-Facebook-or-Yahoo-like
8. Joanna Beltowska, "A Day in the Life of a Product Manager at Pivotal Labs", 16th December 2014, https://medium.com/product-labs/a-day-in-the-life-of-a-product-manager-at-pivotal-labs-ead9149af629
9. Anne-Sophie Lardet, "A day in the life of a Product Manager", 15th September 2016, www.linkedin.com/pulse/day-life-product-manager-anne-sophie-lardet
10. "What's a typical day like for a product manager at Google?", Quora, 6th January 2014, www.quora.com/Whats-a-typical-day-like-for-a-product-manager-at-Google

11. "What is a principal product manager at Amazon?", Quora, 29th December 2016, https://www.quora.com/What-is-a-principal-product-manager-at-Amazon

12. Jack Zenger & Joseph Folkman, "The Skills Leaders Need at Every Level", Harvard Business Review, 30th July 2014, https://hbr.org/2014/07/the-skills-leaders-need-at-every-level

13. Justin Sonnenburg & Erica Sonnenburg, "Gut Feelings–the "Second Brain" in Our Gastrointestinal Systems", Scientific American, 1st May 2015, www.scientificamerican.com/article/gut-feelings-the-second-brain-in-our-gastrointestinal-systems-excerpt. Jennifer Wolkin, "Meet Your Second Brain: The Gut", Mindful.org, 14th August 2015, www.mindful.org/meet-your-second-brain-the-gut/

14. Satya Patel, "What makes a great product manager?", Venture Generated Content, 30th October 2014, https://venturegeneratedcontent.com/2014/10/30/what-makes-a-great-product-manager/

15. Sarah Green Carmichael, "The Research Is Clear: Long Hours Backfire for People and for Companies", Harvard Business Review, 19th August 2015, https://hbr.org/2015/08/the-research-is-clear-long-hours-backfire-for-people-and-for-companies

16. Vicky Webster& Martin Webster, "10 Signs of Micromanagement — Strategies for Dealing With Micromanagers", Leadership Thoughts, www.leadershipthoughts.com/10-signs-of-micromanagement

17. Rebecca Knight, "How to Stop Micromanaging Your Team", Harvard Business Review, 21st August 2015, https://hbr.org/2015/08/how-to-stop-micromanaging-your-team

18. Melissa Perri, "What makes a great Product Manager", 11th January 2015, http://melissaperri.com/2015/01/11/what-makes-a-great-product-manager

19. p40, Outliers, Malcolm Gladwell, Penguin, 2009

20. Mendelow, A. (1991). Stakeholder mapping. Proceedings of the 2nd International Conference on In-formation Systems, Cambridge, MA, 1991 / Fran Ackermann and Colin Eden, p183, "Strategic Management of Stakeholders: Theory and Practice", Long Range Planning, Volume 44, 2011

21. "What It's Like To Work "The Spotify Way", Corporate Rebels, 27th September 2016, https://corporate-rebels.com/spotify-1

22. Rob Cross, Reb Rebele & Adam Grant, "Collaborative Overload", Harvard Business Review, January–February 2016 Issue, https://hbr.org/2016/01/collaborative-overload

23. Chandra Gnanasambandam, Martin Harrysson, Shivam Srivastava & Yun Wu, "Product managers for the digital world", McKinsey & Company, May 2017, www.mckinsey.com/industries/high-tech/our-insights/product-managers-for-the-digital-world

24. Senior Product Manager Job Role, Deliveroo, https://boards.greenhouse.io/deliveroo/jobs/745553#.WpkUQKhl_IU

25. Dan Levin, "The Importance of Mistakes", 28th March 2016, www.linkedin.com/pulse/importance-mistakes-dan-levin?trk=hp-feed-article-title-like

26. Alex Montuschi, Twitter, 30th June 2016, https://twitter.com/montuschi/status/748567906447831040

27. Anderee Berengian, "Innovation Labs – It's time to ditch them", 22nd March 2017, Source: https://venturebeat.com/2017/03/22/its-time-to-ditch-your-innovation-lab